Stuck No More Workbook

Stuck No More Workbook

The Defenses Busters

Dr. Nicki J. Monti

WALLA PRESS

BEVERLY HILLS, CALIFORNIA

© Copyright 2002 by Dr. Nicki J. Monti

All rights reserved.

No part of this book may be reproduced or used in any form or by any means, electronic or mechanical, including photocopying, recording, or by any information storage and retrieval system, without permission in writing from the author.

Address inquiries to:
Dr. Nick J. Monti
269 South Beverly Drive, Suite 430
Beverly Hills, CA 90212

Published by Walla Press
Beverly Hills, CA 90212
Call toll-free: (877) NOT-STUK

www.stucknomore.com

ISBN 0-9723004-0-6

Cover and interior design artwork by Russell Naftal

First Printing: September 2002
Second Printing: January 2003

Printed in the United States of America

The Defense Busters

"Thus is cure a paradox requiring two incommensurables: The moral recognition that these parts of me are burdensome and intolerable and must change, and the loving laughing acceptance which takes them just as they are, joyfully, forever."
— *James Hillman*

CONTENTS

INTRODUCTION 1

Chapter 1. **THE DEFENSE DETECTORS** 5
Probing deeply into the very real ways you've weaved defensive habits into your daily life.

Chapter 2. **THE FOURTEEN SOLUTIONS** 49
Change your old defensive habits with these practical new ways of thinking, feeling, and doing.

Chapter 3. **THE DEFENSE ALTERNATIVES** 79
Specific counter-measures you can apply to particular defenses—and how to apply them!

Chapter 4. **THE DEFENSE RESOURCES** 141
Recognizing and appreciating the genuine value that defenses have had in your life.

AT LAST 165

APPENDIX A: *FIFTEEN STEPS IN DEFENSE BUSTING* 168
APPENDIX B: *CORRELATIONS BY DEFENSE* 170
APPENDIX C: *CORRELATIONS BY SYMPTOM* 172
APPENDIX D: *HEALING PATHWAYS* 174

PUBLISHER'S NOTE

This workbook is a companion to Dr. Nicki J. Monti's foundational book, *Stuck in the Story No More: Breaking Down the Defenses the Define You and Bind You.* By itself, this workbook can be powerfully beneficial. However its value is multiplied many times when you also read *and begin to apply* the fundamental concepts initially presented in *Stuck in the Story No More.*

Together, both books thus offer uniquely comprehensive, practical guidance in understanding the problems that are part of psychological defenses—and how those problems can be solved.

INTRODUCTION

SCREAM PLAYS

Nearly a decade after two brief early marriages (and long before I met my husband Konrad), I began an active search for my "prince." At that point, I (mysteriously) found myself in relationships with all manner of unavailable men. What bad luck, I thought. There were married men aplenty, long-distance romances, and men who could not commit to staying overnight, let alone a lifetime. I was miffed, confused, hurt, and perplexed. I felt let down. Just like at home.

In the midst of these disappointing experiences—and after I had been in the "dating marketplace" for what seemed like an interminable amount of time—I began what seemed like a terrific relationship with, no less, another therapist. He was smart, caring, and available. I thought. No matter that he had a lousy commitment track record. No matter that he too had a couple of marriages under his belt.

After we had been dating for several months, one sweet, casual California evening my beau and I joined a party of friends. I was cradled in my sweetie's arms, my back to him, listening as he purred his revelations to the couple who sat across from us on the floor. "Not since my first wife," he said, "have I felt this way. I've dated many women but have never wanted to make a life with any of them. Now I feel I've met someone so right for me . . . so in sync with me . . . that I must go for it." As these honey words floated over my head, I snuggled in closer, feeling his warm, knowing arms around me.

True, I was slightly surprised. Our conversations and times together had been fun and sexy and close, and surely I entertained the possibility that this relationship might be going somewhere, but the avid feelings he now expressed far exceeded what I might have expected based on my experience with him thus far. And yet I felt content to be so wanted.

That evening as we undressed for bed, lover boy dropped the bomb. Yes, *he had met "Ms. Right,"* which, he explained, was why he had to stop seeing *me*! He went on to explain that he was hopelessly, finally, gratefully in love.

I could hardly believe my ears. Who was this poacher? *I* was Ms. Right! I couldn't believe it was *she* about whom he'd been talking all evening. How could he have held me in his arms while speaking of another?

In the ensuing battle, I righteously ranted and raved. I was furious. I felt betrayed and humiliated. Finally, in the middle of my own ravings, a profound sentence flew out of my mouth and stunned me into silence. The sentence was, "I hate you and *I hate my father.*" I said it as one flowing, unconsidered thought. No reason accompanied my outburst. I was simultaneously forty and four years old when I said it. If we had been on a game show, all the bells and whistles would have sounded at that moment.

And something went *clunk*. Certainly a reasonable measure of disgust for the arrogant thoughtlessness of this self-centered idiot was included in my reaction, but considering what an early stage our relationship was in, the extent and power of my rage was over-the-top. I quickly realized that rage was not for or about *this* man—but, in fact, was for and about the original man . . . Dad.

I knew I needed to sort things out—to understand exactly how the past was still influencing the present. I was tired of feeling like I got hit by a truck every time I stepped off a curb.

Motivated by the weariness that resulted from my own defensiveness and from the life to which that defensiveness had brought me, I began to gather healing ideas and exercises. I drew on my training and experience, on my intuition, and on what I had learned over the years from my various teachers. I conducted a thorough trial-and-error examination of what approaches were successful for and with my clients. I brought together everything I knew—adding what worked, eliminating what didn't, reshaping numerous ideas and exercises, recreating others, and discovering still more, all in an effort to find a workable pathway to healing. (Years later, when I met Konrad, I was able to apply what I'd already figured out, then move even more deeply into the exploration and resolution of my defensive ways.)

The results of that investigation and experience are reflected in this book. And since I realize that different approaches are required for different individuals, you will find a wide range of choices. The trick is to *choose something and use it*. The suggestions and exercises will help only if you actually put them to work in your life.

Some people worry that as they begin to see through a particular defense and eliminate its negative impact, they will veer sharply and uncomfortably in an opposite direction. This is not likely to be a problem, since you have been the way you are for so long that even if you begin exhibiting or engaging in completely opposite behaviors, feelings or thoughts, you will soon swing back to a place of balance. In other words, a withdrawn individual will not turn out to be uncontrollably loquacious, nor will an aggressive individual become timid or fearful. In fact, the challenge you're more likely to encounter is learning how to maintain your new ways in the face of old habits. The idea, then, is to trust yourself (as well as trusting the defenses you have so beautifully developed to keep you in balance and in check) when you're exploring your new thinking, feeling, and behavioral options).

Workout #1

Trust yourself and the defenses you have developed.

This Workbook will address the ways in which you can learn more about your particular defenses, and then how you can begin to do something concrete and positive about those defenses.

With the exercises here suggested, you will be attempting to change both your behavior and your perspective. The procedure is as follows:

❖ Detect the *problem* that underlies your defenses—the situations, attitudes, and teachings that first initiated those defenses.

❖ Learn real, vital *solutions* for change,

❖ Begin to *practice* the *alternative* actions that those solutions call for.

By the way, just in case after following my three-part procedural plan, you begin to feel as though you've wasted your whole life being defensive, you will come to (happily) realize that in your years of defensiveness, you've actually acquired some terrific skills along the way.

❖ Your fourth procedural step then will be to acknowledge the various resources that can now ably support a healthier life for you.

Follow this path and be stuck in the story no more.

CHAPTER 1

THE DEFENSE DETECTORS

To the detectives

Your investigation will give you a chance now to ask very specific questions about the defenses you have thus far identified as your own. (Or, if you are trying to understand the behavior of a family member, friend, or coworker, you may want to apply these questions to them.) Look through this chapter, find the defenses you previously recognized as being of special interest to you, and answer the questions that refer to those particular defenses. The answers you give will provide you with further insight into that defense.

The questions here are preliminary and are intended to provoke the probing that will help you unravel the deeper mystery of your own behavior. The rules for answering these questions and for initiating that probing are easy to follow—though they are sometimes difficult to honor. Those rules are:

- ❖ When answering questions, *do not* over-think. There is no *right* answer, so *don't* get hung up on trying to be correct.
- ❖ Allow yourself to be surprised by what you discover. Some of your most important answers may seem amazingly simple—even perhaps *too* simple to

satisfy you. Nevertheless, resist the temptation to disregard them because of this simplicity. In this exercise, "simple" probably means clear—and that is good.

- ❖ Try not to berate yourself for not having arrived at this apparently obvious understanding before. Answers only come when you are ready. Compliment yourself for being ready now.
- ❖ Attempt to ignore the part of you that wants everything to make sense right away. What's important at this juncture is merely to gather information, without worrying about what it all means. Try to appreciate (and even to enjoy) the information-gathering process itself, without focusing on how it will turn out.
- ❖ Before you begin to write the answers to the questions, take a moment to focus your attention on what you're doing. One extremely useful technique is to focus for 30-60 seconds on your breathing. Now close your eyes and repeat to yourself several times a key word—such as the word or words that describe the defense you are working on. Thus, with each breath you might say: *anger, anger, anger.* Now write your answers, letting the words flow unselfconsciously onto the page.

Note: To help you get into this work more easily, directly, and quickly, I have provided space on each of the following pages where you can respond to the questions and suggestions that appear. However, I enthusiastically suggest that you to look far beyond the space available in those few lines and that you write freely, extensively, and prolifically—in order to reveal to yourself the fullness of your inner workings.

HIT DEFENSES: CONNECTION THROUGH FEELING

The defense of ANGER
Protecting yourself with feelings of hostility.

①

What kinds of situations stimulate your anger? (Be specific: waiter ignores me, mate leaves toothpaste cap off, mother criticizes me.) What actions are you likely to take under these circumstances?

_____

_____

②

List some of the phrases you frequently say (out loud or in your head) about or to others when you are angry.

_____

_____

③

If you weren't feeling anger, what might you be feeling instead? Explain.

_____

_____

④

Write about the ways in which anger controls your life.

_____

_____

HIT DEFENSES: CONNECTION THROUGH FEELING

The defense of CONTEMPT FOR OTHERS

Protecting yourself with despising, negative, disdainful feelings toward other people.

①

How does contempt feel to you and what kinds of things do you say out loud or in your head when you feel this way? (She's a dog, what an imbecile he is, I don't know how he ever got hired, I can't believe someone so stupid can get so far!)

_____

_____

②

What kinds of people and situations most often inspire your contempt?

_____

_____

③

What do you usually do when you are feeling contemptuous? (I keep it to myself, which makes me feel [how/what?], I show it by [doing/saying what?], I tell other people how I feel by saying [what?].)

_____

_____

④

Write about the way your contempt for others affects your relationships.

_____

_____

HIT DEFENSES: CONNECTION THROUGH FEELING

The defense of BLAME
Protecting yourself by feeling and believing that someone else is at fault.

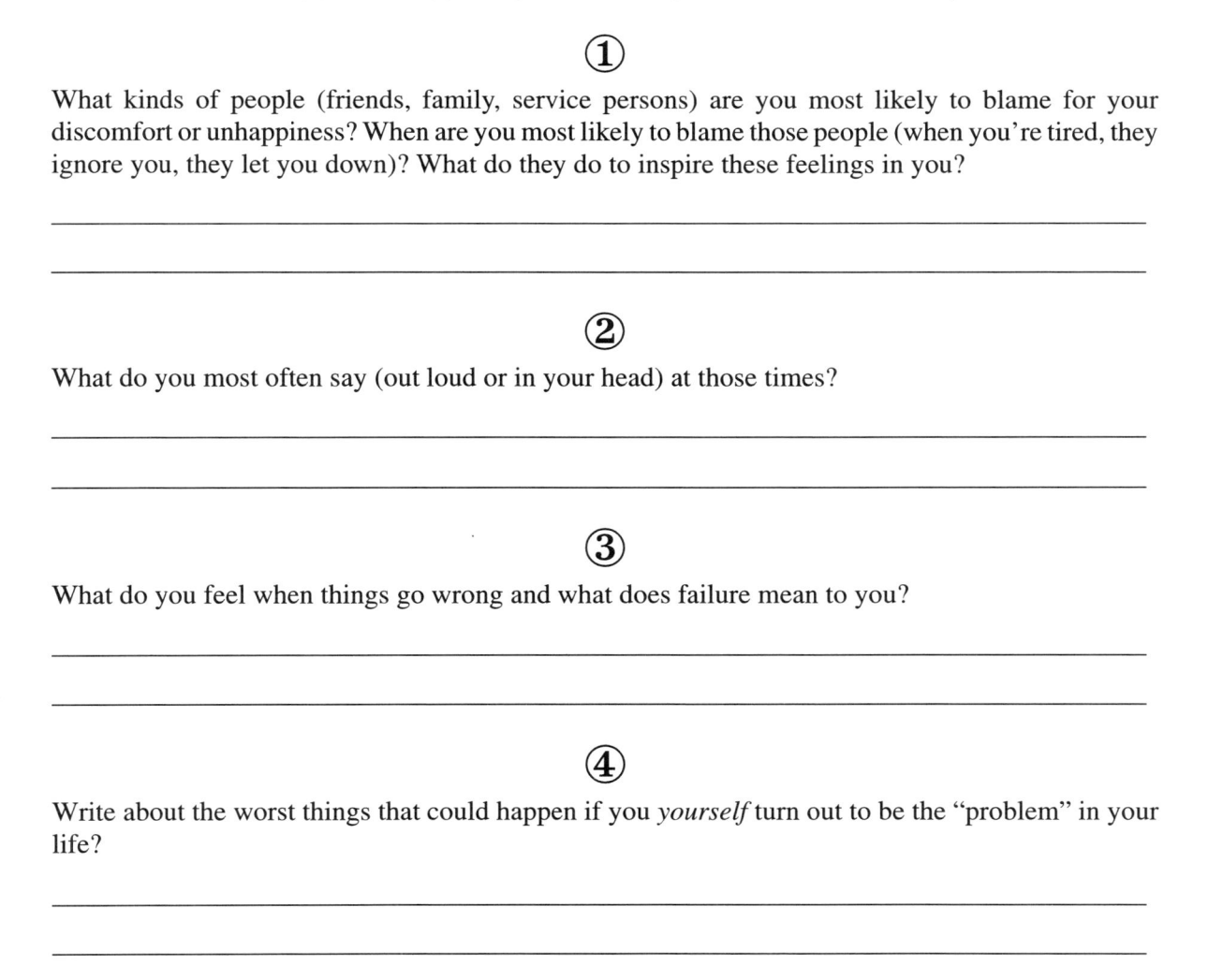

①
What kinds of people (friends, family, service persons) are you most likely to blame for your discomfort or unhappiness? When are you most likely to blame those people (when you're tired, they ignore you, they let you down)? What do they do to inspire these feelings in you?

_____

_____

②
What do you most often say (out loud or in your head) at those times?

_____

_____

③
What do you feel when things go wrong and what does failure mean to you?

_____

_____

④
Write about the worst things that could happen if you *yourself* turn out to be the "problem" in your life?

_____

_____

HIT DEFENSES: CONNECTION THROUGH DOING

The defense of SPILLING
Protecting yourself with constant (often inappropriate) talking.

①
While you're talking, what are you thinking and what are you feeling?

_____

_____

②
What do you imagine to be the aim of your conversations?

_____

_____

③
What feelings or thoughts come up when you're silent or say much less than usual?

_____

_____

④
Write about your feelings of disconnectedness from others or from the world.

_____

_____

HIT DEFENSES: CONNECTION THROUGH DOING

The defense of GOSSIP

Protecting yourself by talking to someone about someone else who is not present.

①

What are your favorite gossip topics and with whom is gossip most fun (be specific)? How do you feel after you have gossiped about someone? What happens inside you when next you meet the person you gossiped about?

_____

_____

②

When you don't gossip, what do you talk about?

_____

_____

③

Who gossips about *you* and what do they say (or what do you think they say)?

_____

_____

④

Write about how gossip keeps you from sharing (intimate) things about yourself?

_____

_____

HIT DEFENSES: CONNECTION THROUGH DOING

The defense of HUMOR

Protecting yourself with comical (sometimes inappropriate) self-expression.

①

In what situations and for what kinds of people do you most often turn to humor, and what does that expression of humor usually look like (for example, flippancy, sarcasm or . . .)?

_____

_____

②

How do other people generally react to your expressions of humor?

_____

_____

③

When you were growing up, how was humor exhibited in your home?

_____

_____

④

Write about the circumstances in which, and the kinds of people with whom, you feel most vulnerable. How does that vulnerability impact you, and what do you think would happen if you "gave in" to it?

_____

_____

HIT DEFENSES: CONNECTION THROUGH DOING

The defense of DEPENDENCE
Protecting yourself through excessive reliance on others.

①

Who helps you most in your life and what kinds of things do he/she/they do? (Mother sends you money once a month, roommate drives you to work in the mornings, partner handles all of your money.)

_____

_____

②

Suppose the assistance you are now receiving were discontinued. What do you think would happen to you?

_____

_____

③

In what situations and with what kinds of people do you feel most powerless, small, and/or helpless?

_____

_____

④

Write about what you think would need to happen for you to become independent.

_____

_____

HIT DEFENSES: CONNECTION THROUGH DOING

The defense of CODEPENDENCE
Protecting yourself through excessive reliance on people or things to define your self-worth.

①

What ways of helping people do you most commonly use? With whom are you most likely to use these methods? When and with whom is it hardest for you to say no? What *thoughts* or *feelings* come up for you when you do say no?

_____

_____

②

How do you think other people view you? What feelings and thoughts come up when you think someone doesn't like you?

_____

_____

③

Keep a written record of how much private and/or alone time you have each day. What kinds of things do you do *only* for yourself?

_____

_____

④

Write about what you think will happen if you stop doing so much for other people.

_____

_____

HIT DEFENSES: CONNECTION THROUGH DOING

The defense of THERAPIZING
Protecting yourself through excessive (often unrequested) advice-giving.

①

What kinds of people are most likely to lean on you for advice? How do you feel when you are advising them?

_____

_____

②

About what kinds of things are you most likely to advise, interpret, counsel, or comment? How do people usually respond to you when you do those things?

_____

_____

③

What other benefits and rewards do you offer your friends and acquaintances besides those of help and problem-solving?

_____

_____

④

Who was the authority in your house when you were growing up? How did that work? Write about the advantages of being the authority now.

_____

_____

HIT DEFENSES: CONNECTION THROUGH DOING

The defense of CONTROL
Protecting yourself by exercising a regulating or directing influence.

①

Notice the feelings and thoughts that arise when you are not in charge and when things don't go your way.

_____

_____

②

List the kinds of situations and/or people you feel obligated to manage and what you think would happen if you were not in control of those situations and/or people?

_____

_____

③

Exactly what "take charge" things do you do?

_____

_____

④

Write about the time when you first discovered your need to be in charge.

_____

_____

HIT DEFENSES: CONNECTION THROUGH DOING

The defense of CRITICISM
Protecting yourself by constantly finding fault.

①

What characteristics in other people do you find most irritating, and what kinds of people most often exhibit these characteristics?

_____

_____

②

What is the general nature of your criticism and how does it affect others?

_____

_____

③

What are the things about which you most often criticize yourself and what are the ways in which do so?

_____

_____

④

Write about incompetence—what you think of it, how other people's incompetence affects you, and what you think will happen if you relax your critical vigilance.

_____

_____

HIT DEFENSES: CONNECTION THROUGH THINKING

The defense of PROJECTION
Protecting yourself by using other people as a screen for unconscious thoughts and feelings.

①
At work, at play, with friends, with family—how do you think people view you (be specific)?

_____

_____

②
What kinds of people do you think are most judgmental of you, and what (specifically) do you believe those people think about you?

_____

_____

③
What were you told (and shown) about yourself when you were growing up?

_____

_____

④
Write about your fears of being seen as the person you really are.

_____

_____

HIT DEFENSES: CONNECTION THROUGH THINKING

The defense of JUDGMENT
Protecting yourself with opinions that tend to be moral, critical, or righteous.

①

Under what circumstances are you most likely to express your judgments about others? What specific things do you usually say?

_____
_____

②

Identify the characteristics in others about which you tend to be most critical (for instance: incompetence, unreliability, lying). How do these things show up in you? (Remember that these characteristics will seldom appear in you exactly the way they look in other people—"My brother has no ambition. I can't commit to relationships.)

_____
_____

③

What are the things about which you most often judge yourself, and what are the ways in which these judgments affect your life.

_____
_____

④

Write about your rules for living. What are they, how do they work and to whom do they apply?

_____
_____

HIT DEFENSES: CONNECTION THROUGH THINKING

The defense of COMPARING
Protecting yourself by measuring the way you feel against the way others appear.

①

Under what circumstances and with what kinds of people are you most likely to compare yourself? Do you most often feel better than or inferior to others? In what way?

_____

_____

②

What about yourself (or your life) do you wish were different?

_____

_____

③

How did your parents talk to you and to friends about other people?

_____

_____

④

Assume that you and another person have an authentically intimate connection. Write about the fears that arise in you in regard to this intimacy.

_____

_____

HIT DEFENSES: CONNECTION THROUGH THINKING

The defense of ANALYZING

Protecting yourself by measuring the way you feel against the way others appear.

①

When did you first realize you were good at figuring things out?

___

②

Who are your favorite people (individuals or groups) to analyze? Under what circumstances do you usually do such analysis? How do people respond to your scrutiny? What's your reaction when others analyze *you*?

___

③

Do you think unexpressed emotions affect you? If so, how?

___

④

Write about what you do when nonrational thoughts occur to you. What feelings are easiest for you to acknowledge in yourself and what feelings are most disturbing to acknowledge in others.

___

HIT DEFENSES: CONNECTION THROUGH THINKING

The defense of MASKING
Protecting yourself by saying one thing while feeling or thinking another.

①
Around what kinds of people (relatives, associates, strangers, authority figures) do you feel you need to be most "careful"? What kinds of things do you do to protect yourself?

_____

_____

②
What things are you most afraid that others will find out about you?

_____

_____

③
What are some of the methods you use most often to maintain secrecy?

_____

_____

④
Write about the "real" you: what you would *say* if you could tell the truth and how you think that would change your relationships; what you would *do* if you were following your heart and how you think that would change your life.

_____

_____

RUN DEFENSES: DISCONNECTION THROUGH FEELING

The defense of SHAME
Protecting yourself through your all-pervasive sense of basic defectiveness.

①

Under what circumstances are you most self-conscious, and what are the self-defeating phrases you most frequently say (to yourself or to others)?

___

___

②

When are you most likely to shame others and who are you most likely to shame? What form does that shaming take?

___

___

③

Which members of your family (present or past) do you regard as the *most* shaming and/or shameful. How and why?

___

___

④

Write about what you imagine your life would be like if it were shame-free.

___

___

RUN DEFENSES: DISCONNECTION THROUGH FEELING

The defense of SELF-CONTEMPT
Protecting yourself by using excessive expressions of self-disdain.

①
What demeaning thoughts do you have about yourself and what self-denigrating things do you say out loud.

_____

_____

②
What are your areas of greatest self-contempt. What situations and/or kinds of people are most likely to inspire this self-contempt?

_____

_____

③
How do you think your self-contempt impacts your relationships?

_____

_____

④
Write about how your life would be different if you were free of self-contempt.

_____

_____

RUN DEFENSES: DISCONNECTION THROUGH FEELING

The defense of FEAR
Protecting yourself through persistent feelings of eminent (emotional or physical) danger.

①
Under what circumstances are you most afraid?

_____

_____

②
When do you first remember these circumstances being in your life?

_____

_____

③
What are you most likely to do when you are afraid?

_____

_____

④
Write about the ways in which fear inhibits your life?

_____

_____

RUN DEFENSES: DISCONNECTION THROUGH FEELING

The defense of VICTIM

Protecting yourself by focusing on feeling cheated, fooled, abused, or ignored by people and/or circumstances.

①
When do you feel most victimized, and how do you usually respond?
_____
_____

②
Who in your life is most likely to "come to the rescue," and exactly what is that rescue like?
_____
_____

③
List all the "horrible" things that have happened to you in the last 10 years.
_____
_____

④
Write with rigorous honesty about *your* contribution to the above-listed "horrible" experiences (my husband abused me, but I didn't leave; I had to declare bankruptcy because I didn't pay close attention to my finances; my spouse had an affair, but even before it happened, I failed to talk about the distance that had been growing up between us).
_____
_____

RUN DEFENSES: DISCONNECTION THROUGH FEELING

The defense of WITHDRAWAL
Protecting yourself through emotional and even physical retreat.

①
Under what circumstances and with what kinds of people do you most want to hide out?

___

___

②
What kinds of things do you think and feel when you're with others and they're talking but you're not?

___

___

③
When in your life did you start separating yourself from others, and (these days) what methods do you most often use to achieve this separation?

___

___

④
Write about your fear of *visibility* and also about what you think would happen if people found out what you're thinking and feeling.

___

___

RUN DEFENSES: DISCONNECTION THROUGH FEELING

The defense of DEPRESSION
Protecting yourself through feelings of emotional, mental, and/or physical paralysis.

①
What thoughts go through your head when you're depressed?

_____

_____

②
When you're depressed, how do you behave differently in your life? How do people treat you at those times?

_____

_____

③
When do you first remember being depressed? What was going on in your life?

_____

_____

④
Write about what you think would happen if you were to express *all* of your feelings.

_____

_____

RUN DEFENSES: DISCONNECTION THROUGH FEELING

The defense of TERMINAL UNIQUENESS

Protecting yourself through your feelings of being completely different from other people and through your ideas that you are therefore misperceived by them.

①

Under what circumstances and with what kinds of people are you most likely to feel separate, different, and left out? What do you usually do at those times?

_____

_____

②

When did you first begin thinking you didn't fit in? Why?

_____

_____

③

What do you think are your most unique qualities? How are you ordinary or much like others.

_____

_____

④

Write about loneliness. When do you feel the loneliest, when did it begin, and how did it affect your life?

_____

_____

RUN DEFENSES: DISCONNECTION THROUGH FEELING

The defense of SPIRITUALITY

Protecting yourself through the use of excessive religious or spiritual referencing.

①

With whom and under what circumstances are you most likely to discuss spiritual ideas (atheists, people of like mind, family members . . . at social gatherings, at religious services, at home)?

_____

_____

②

How do you feel when people reject your spiritual teachings?

_____

_____

③

When were you first aware of being spiritual? Describe what was going on in your life at that time?

_____

_____

④

Write about the times you lose your faith.

_____

_____

RUN DEFENSES: DISCONNECTION THROUGH DOING

The defense of CHAOS
Protecting yourself through vast, disordered confusion.

①
What form does the chaos in your life take, and how do you feel when that chaos is occurring?

_____

_____

②
What were your earliest experiences of chaos?

_____

_____

③
What do you do to maintain the chaos in your life? Be specific (refuse to organize your possessions, am constantly late, can never find anything)

_____

_____

④
Write about your earliest experiences of chaos. What do you suspect would happen if harmony replaced disorder?

_____

_____

RUN DEFENSES: DISCONNECTION THROUGH DOING

The defense of COMPULSIVITY

Protecting yourself through impulsive, repetitious, self-defeating behavior.

①

What actions do you continue to take in your daily life, even though you know they are counterproductive or are absorbing more time and energy than they should (working too many hours, watching too much TV, eating too much)? What do you say to yourself when you behave in these unhealthy ways?

_____

_____

②

Does your life feel balanced? If not, what's missing?

_____

_____

③

What are the circumstances in your life about which you feel most frustrated or discontented? What would you need to do to change those circumstances?

_____

_____

④

Write about what you think would happen if people knew how sensitive you really are. Which feelings are you most anxious to avoid?

_____

_____

RUN DEFENSES: DISCONNECTION THROUGH DOING

The defense of COUNTER-DEPENDENCE
Protecting yourself through stubborn self-reliance.

①
When and with whom are you most impatient? What kinds of people do you find to be most undependable?

_____

_____

②
What thoughts and feelings occur to you when you consider asking for help? ("It would take longer to explain this than to do it myself." "No one can help me anyway.")

_____

_____

③
When was the first time in your life you remember being let down and, as a result, deciding to take charge?

_____

_____

④
Write about what you think will happen if you stop working so hard, let go of some of your fierce independence, and start relying on others in significant ways?

_____

_____

RUN DEFENSES: DISCONNECTION THROUGH DOING

The defense of PROCRASTINATION

Protecting yourself by putting things off until the last minute.

①

What kinds of things do you put off until the last minute, and how do you feel when you put these things off?

_____

_____

②

How do other people respond to your procrastinating ways? How does that response make you feel?

_____

_____

③

Do you think you're more afraid of success or of failure? Why?

_____

_____

④

Write about the effects of procrastination on your life.

_____

_____

RUN DEFENSES: DISCONNECTION THROUGH DOING

The defense of WITHHOLDING
Protecting yourself by holding back emotionally and/or physically.

①
Under what circumstances and with whom are you most unwilling to engage in conversation? How long do you usually continue this disengagement and what do you think about or feel during your silence?

_____

_____

②
If you were not holding back at all, what would you be saying and to whom?

_____

_____

③
Who or what do you think you're most angry at or frustrated with? What first initiated those feelings? What perpetuates them?

_____

_____

④
Write about your fear of telling your truth and of the visibility that goes with that telling.

_____

_____

RUN DEFENSES: DISCONNECTION THROUGH DOING

The defense of PHYSICAL ILLNESS
Protecting yourself through constant, nagging, repetitive experiences of body problems.

①
How often do you get sick and what is your usual response to getting sick?

_____

_____

②
How do others treat you when you're ill?

_____

_____

③
The next time you're sick, list the significant physical, emotional, and mental events that occurred in the twenty-four hours before you got sick. Do this each subsequent time you are ill.

_____

_____

④
Write about ways other than illness in which you give yourself permission to slow down.

_____

_____

RUN DEFENSES: DISCONNECTION THROUGH DOING

The defense of DISSOCIATION

Protecting yourself through an emotional separation from everything and everyone—including separation from your own physical self.

①

Under what circumstances and with what kinds of individuals do you most often find yourself feeling disconnected physically and/or mentally? What does that disconnection feel like (include physical sensations)?

_____

_____

②

When do you remember feeling numb, "out of your body," or as though you were "watching yourself"? What happened?

_____

_____

③

What specific feelings do you suspect you'd be having if you weren't dissociating?

_____

_____

④

Write about what you think might happen if you were completely connected (to yourself and others) through passionate feelings.

_____

_____

RUN DEFENSES: DISCONNECTION THROUGH THINKING

The defense of PARANOIA

Protecting yourself by assuming that people and/or circumstances are against you.

①

Where, how, and when are you most likely to feel threatened (by inner or outer things, people, or circumstances)?

_____

_____

②

What (negative) thoughts and feelings do you believe other people have about you?

_____

_____

③

When you feel others are against you, what are you most likely to do?

_____

_____

④

Write about the ways in which you think your exceptional vigilance affects your relationships?

_____

_____

RUN DEFENSES: DISCONNECTION THROUGH THINKING

The defense of GUILT
Protecting yourself by thinking you have done a bad thing.

①
When and with whom do you feel most apologetic?

_____

_____

②
What kinds of things do you say (to yourself or to others) when you think you've "done something wrong"?

_____

_____

③
If you were not feeling guilty, what kinds of feelings do you suspect you'd be having?

_____

_____

④
Write about the specific ways in which guilt undermines both your relationships to other people and your appreciation for your own good work. Note the results of that undermining.

_____

_____

RUN DEFENSES: DISCONNECTION THROUGH THINKING

The defense of CONFUSION
Protecting yourself through emotional and/or intellectual ambivalence and disorder.

①
When do you feel most confused or overwhelmed? What is usually the result that feeling?

_____

_____

②
How do others respond to you when you are confused?

_____

_____

③
How do you think confusion impedes your progress.

_____

_____

④
Write about the confusion you experienced in your family when you were growing up.

_____

_____

RUN DEFENSES: DISCONNECTION THROUGH THINKING

The defense of INTELLECTUALIZATION
Protecting yourself through excessive analyzing, pondering, mapping, exploring, and investigating.

①

Under what circumstances do you feel the smartest? With what types of people does your mind work "best"?

_____

_____

②

How do you think intellectualizing affects your relationships?

_____

_____

③

What reaction are you likely to have if you do not have the time or energy to think things through?

_____

_____

④

Write about *feelings*: particularly which ones are most unacceptable to you? Describe people who exhibit strong feelings—what do you think about them and how do you treat them?

_____

_____

RUN DEFENSES: DISCONNECTION THROUGH THINKING

The defense of DENIAL
Protecting yourself by refusing to accept (an obvious) truth.

①
What things have people told you about yourself that you disbelieve? How do you feel when they describe you in a way that doesn't make sense to you?

_____
_____

②
What are the areas of your life in which you feel stuck?

_____
_____

③
When you see denial in others, what does it look like?

_____
_____

④
Write about what you imagine would happen if you took to heart other people's suggestions regarding your behavior.

_____
_____

RUN DEFENSES: DISCONNECTION THROUGH THINKING

The defense of SKEPTICISM

Protecting yourself through excessive, pervasive negativity and doubt.

①

About what topics are you most skeptical?

_____

_____

②

Under what circumstances and with what kinds of people is your skepticism most likely to erupt?

_____

_____

③

What kinds of things do you say when you're feeling skeptical?

_____

_____

④

Write about what you think happens to people who "take things on faith."

_____

_____

RUN DEFENSES: DISCONNECTION THROUGH THINKING

The defense of OBSESSION

*Protecting yourself through repetitive focus on an idea, feeling, person, or thing—
a focus that most often overrides all other thinking.*

①

What kinds of thoughts preoccupy you, how do you behave when you feel preoccupied and how does that preoccupation affect those around you?

_____

_____

②

What relieves your preoccupation?

_____

_____

③

If you weren't preoccupied, what would be different in your life?

_____

_____

④

Write about the areas and ways in which obsession rules your life.

_____

_____

RUN DEFENSES: DISCONNECTION THROUGH THINKING

The defense of SELF-ABSORPTION
Protecting yourself through excessive self-centeredness.

①
When do you feel most important?

_____

_____

②
What kinds of thoughts and feelings do you have when people talk about themselves?

_____

_____

③
What happens to you when you are ignored, overlooked, denied, or rejected?

_____

_____

④
Write about the quality and quantity of attention you got when you were growing up.

_____

_____

RUN DEFENSES: DISCONNECTION THROUGH THINKING

The defense of FANTASY
Protecting yourself through a preoccupation with illusory notions.

①
When do you tend to daydream most (list circumstances and times) and what is the overall nature of your favorite fantasies?

_____

_____

②
How do you feel after you have finished a fantasy experience?

_____

_____

③
As a child, on what occasions or in what situations were you most likely to fantasize? At these times, what did you fantasize about?

_____

_____

④
Write about your disappointment over the realities of your life.

_____

_____

RUN DEFENSES: DISCONNECTION THROUGH THINKING

The defense of PERFECTIONISM
Protecting yourself by insisting upon <u>excessively</u> high standards.

①
In what areas are you hardest on yourself? On others?

_____

_____

②
What kinds of things do you tell yourself about making mistakes?

_____

_____

③
What precisely are your ways of exhibiting your perfectionism (meticulous cleaning, extremely controlled eating, excessive planning)?

_____

_____

④
Write about the lack of safety you feel with other people and in the world—when it started and how it feels now.

_____

_____

CHAPTER 2

THE FOURTEEN SOLUTIONS

Aunt Emma

Change comes when we can see what has been, what is, and what can be in an entirely new light. This means a *fundamental shift in perspective.* I remember such an alteration occurring for me many years ago, during my undergraduate years at the University of Wisconsin. At that time I often frequented country auctions and at one such event I obtained the portrait I declared to be "Aunt Emma." Something about Emma in her gently tinted, thirties, plain metal-framed photograph drew me in.

For years, Aunt Emma followed me from home to home and from state to state. Often, I would gaze at her proud, still countenance . . . her almost disdainful expression. I saw her sitting, as it were, looking critically down on me and my travails.

Then, perhaps fifteen years later, I was passing by Emma one day when I suddenly stopped dead in my tracks. I looked carefully at the picture, stunned. Had her expression actually changed? For at that moment, the proud lady appeared rather more amused than stern, more conspiratorial than disdainful. Where had all her arrogance gone?

It did not take me long to figure out that *Emma had not changed*. The only thing I was left to conclude was that my "vision" had so altered that Emma *looked changed*. I saw clearly in that moment the power and impact of perception. I understood completely that *what we see filters through our emotional screens*. Thus, a new world view can actually metamorphose material appearance so that faces look changed and what or who attracts us is different. What has previously seemed ordinary, becomes extraordinary. It's as if we are seeing for the first time.

Accomplishing this shift involves more than understanding concepts. It takes a consistent *intention* to change (attitude), coupled with sincere *effort* (action). The good news is it can be done. True and lasting change can actually occur. We can remember our stories, understand them—even appreciate them—and still free ourselves from a lifelong stuckness. What is seemingly fixed becomes mutable—a photograph frozen in time melts and morphs.

The facts

Your personal *Defense Profile* has revealed what defenses you use most often, how you use those defenses, and how those defenses relate to your life—past and present. Now your work involves breaking free from the old ideas and habits that go with those defenses.

Breaking free

How do you break free? Here are fourteen *alternate* ways for you to think and behave—new responses to old feelings. If you employ these alternatives you will—sometimes slowly, sometimes quickly—find your life changing.

Be aware that the changes you make are likely to lead to the emergence of feelings and/or thoughts you have previously resisted or rejected. Your first temptation may be to resist or reject those thoughts and feelings again. However, you will get more mileage out of facing them instead and—through writing, rumination, and conversation with others—dealing directly with whatever arises.

The 14 solutions build self-esteem (high self-regard).

Self-esteem, though essential to a healthy life, is often misinterpreted as arrogance, contempt, snobbishness, or feigned superiority. "Don't toot your own horn," you are told. "After all, modesty becomes you." However, a good self-concept is not absurd, disproportionate self-approval; it is, rather, a belief in yourself that manifests in positivity, clarity, proactivity, and security.

The 14 solutions offer hope for lasting change.

They are practical, providing you with an opportunity to experience immediate results. Immediate results give you temporary faith, which leads to permanent change.

The 14 solutions teach effective boundary-setting.

Establishing both emotional and physical borders is essential. These borders will allow you to feel safe enough to exhibit and to invite real intimacy.

The 14 solutions teach assertiveness.

Once you feel safe within the boundaries you have set, you will be able to declare what your desires are—what you want and need. The more clearly you express your desires, the more likely you are to get those desires fulfilled.

The 14 solutions teach authentic expressions of vulnerability.

Finally, what you desire (and deserve) in your life are good relationships that support you to feel good about yourself. Such relationships can only be built on authentically expressed feelings.

FOURTEEN SOLUTIONS FOR COPING WITH OR NEUTRALIZING DEFENSIVENESS

Before studying the solutions in detail, scan this quick reference to get a few clues about which ones will be useful for you. See Appendix B and Appendix C for correlations by defense and by symptom.

DEFENSES	SYMPTOMS	SOLUTION
Analyzing, Anger, Chaos, Compulsivity, Dissociation, Fantasy, Fear, Gossip, Humor, Obsession, Paranoia, Perfectionism, Spilling, Therapizing	panic, anxiety, extreme reactivity, nervousness, talkativeness, hyperactivity, clumsiness	#1 **Breathe & Center**
All defenses (and their accompanying characteristics) that reinforce Self-Contempt	all symptoms	#2 **Rouse**
All defenses	all symptoms	#3 **Meditate**
All defenses	all symptoms	#4 **Write**
Chaos, Confusion, Dissociation, Fear, Masking	flightiness, clumsiness, forgetfulness, disjointedness, flakiness, babbling	#5 **Be Here Now**
Blame, Comparing, Contempt, Criticism, Denial, Fantasy, Fear, Guilt, Humor, Intellectualization, Judgment, Obsession, Paranoia, Physical Illness, Self-Absorption, Self-Contempt, Skepticism, Victim	vigilance, panic, over-analyzing, anxiety	#6 **Thought Stop**
Blame, Chaos, Compulsion, Contempt, Gossip, Humor, Intellectualization, Perfectionism, Rage, Shame, Skepticism, Spilling, Spirituality	intrusiveness, babbling, convincing, hyperactivity, nervousness, impulsivity, extreme reactivity, irrationality, snide remarks, talkativeness, tantrums	#7 **Contain**
Anger, Compulsivity, Gossip, Perfectionism, Spirituality	people-pleasing, convincing, boundarilessness, hyperactivity, intrusiveness	#8 **Disengage**

DEFENSES	SYMPTOMS	SOLUTION
Analyzing, Chaos, Codependence, Compulsivity, Confusion, Control, Denial, Dependence, Fantasy, Guilt, Obsession, Paranoia, Perfectionism, Physical Illness, Projection, Self-Absorption, Self-Contempt, Shame, Skepticism, Therapizing, Victim	isolating, reluctance, condescension, lying, over-analyzing, reluctance, sabotage	#9 Get It
Anger, Depression, Fear, Withdrawal, Withholding	hesitation, shyness, discomfort	#10 State the Obvious
Blame, Codependence, Confusion, Control, Criticism, Dependence, Dissociation, Guilt, Intellectualization, Judgment, Masking, Obsession, Perfectionism, Procrastination, Skepticism, Spilling, Spirituality, Terminal Uniqueness, Withholding	people-pleasing, isolating, lying, fantasizing, numbing, covert behavior	#11 Tell the Truth
Analyzing, Confusion, Counter-Dependence, Depression, Fantasy, Gossip, Judgment, Masking, Physical Illness, Procrastination, Projection, Self-Contempt, Shame, Spirituality, Withdrawal	hesitation, shyness, silence, reluctance, boundarilessness	#12 Confront
Nearly all defenses could use a dose of Contrary Action.	almost all symptoms	#13 Take Contrary Action
Comparing, Confusion, Counter-Dependence, Dependence, Depression, Dissociation, Judgment, Self-Absorption, Shame, Victim, Withholding	hesitation, reservation, sabotage, lethargy, flightiness, whining	#14 Get Moving

THE SOLUTIONS

(In categories that show when they will probably meet your needs)

ALWAYS GREAT

Always Great solutions. These solutions are for *everyone* to use on a daily basis. Practiced with consistency they allow you to experience a better overall feeling about your life. The solutions are *Breathe & Center*, *Rouse*, *Meditate,* and *Write*.

Solution #1: **BREATHE & CENTER**
Attaining focus through conscious inhalation & exhalation.

Solution #2: **ROUSE**
Reinforcing your self-esteem through positive self-talk.

Solution #3: **MEDITATE**
Taking quiet time to explore your inner world.

Solution #4: **WRITE**
Putting your thoughts on paper.

GOOD WHEN LESS IS MORE

Good When Less-Is-More solutions. These solutions are for people who, need to learn to speak in a succinct, clear manner (like spillers and compulsives). They get you back in your body, help stop your negative or chaotic thinking, contain your unhealthy behavior and free you from reactivity. They include *Be Here Now*, *Thought Stop*, *Contain,* and *Disengage*.

Solution #5: **BE HERE NOW**
Coming down to earth through mental concentration.

Solution #6: **THOUGHT STOP**
Interrupting unhealthy thinking.

Solution #7: **CONTAIN**
Holding back the emotional and/or physical excesses in your life.

Solution #8: **DISENGAGE**
Releasing yourself from anything that emotionally ensnares you.

GOOD WHEN MORE IS BETTER

Good When More-Is-Better solutions. These solutions teach you to step up and to speak up—to say what you think and reveal what you feel. They include *Get It, State the Obvious, Tell the Truth* and *Confront*.

Solution #9: **GET IT**
Taking a fresh, honest look at yourself.

Solution #10: **STATE THE OBVIOUS**
Saying out loud exactly what you're thinking in the moment.

Solution #11: **TELL THE TRUTH**
*Telling other people what you truly think and feel **about yourself**.*

Solution #12: **CONFRONT**
The clear and suitable expression of your moment-to-moment feelings.

GOOD WHEN ACTION IS NEEDED

Good when action is needed solutions. These last two solutions are about becoming proactive in order to *create* the life you want. They include *Take Contrary Action* and *Get Moving*.

Solution #13: **TAKE CONTRARY ACTION**
Doing the opposite of what you have been doing.

Solution #14: **GET MOVING**
Adding new emotionally and/or physically healthy activities to your daily life.

FOLLOW THE YELLOW BRICK ROAD

Each of these solutions includes **The Intention** (a brief description of the Solution's objective) and **The Mechanics** (the how-to of the Solution). Here is a concise overview of the categories:

"ALWAYS GREAT" SOLUTIONS

Solution #1
Breathe & Center

Attaining focus through conscious inhalation and exhalation.

The Intention: Breathing is a unique function. It's usually automatic, but it can also be immediately and consciously regulated. If you feel scattered or out of control, you can almost always calm yourself by *using* your breath. At times, breathing consciously will provide you with instant evidence of your authority to control yourself and your reactions. At other times, breathing can be used to release and express pent-up feelings.

Whether you are calming down or opening up, conscious breathing is a simple, *completely personal* technique you can use anywhere, anytime, in order to:

- promote inner calm;
- expand your ability to concentrate;
- force your attention onto present feelings and current situations;
- relieve the inner turmoil associated with feeling out of control;
- relax so you can better organize your thoughts;
- relieve your obsessive thinking;
- release your repressed feelings.

The Mechanics: Focus your attention on the center of your upper body, 4"-5" below your throat, on the breastbone. Open your mouth slightly and, with your inner sense, feel your breath go in your nose and down into your lungs as you inhale, and then out your mouth as you exhale. Concentrate on the inward/outward flow of breath. *See* the breath in your mind. *Feel* the breath.

While attempting to focus in this way, you may find yourself tempted to explore irrelevant thoughts ("What shall I have for dinner"; or "I hate the way Tom spoke to me yesterday"). The idea is to keep as clear a mind as possible but when and if extraneous thoughts start to intrude, do not use your energy or attention to keep them away. Instead, simply *observe* the thoughts, without getting involved with them, let those thoughts move through your mind like a gentle wind rustles through the trees. See the thoughts rustle through, but resist the urge to develop or explore them. Continue to concentrate on the inward/outward flow of your breath.

Repeat this exercise as often as necessary . . . until you experience a feeling of calm. If circumstances are appropriate, let yourself drift into the deeper inner realm known as the *meditative* state.

Solution #2
Rouse

Reinforcing your self-esteem through positive self-talk.

The Intention: Rousing intends to replace negative inner chatter with positive inner reinforcement. It is a good parenting procedure, that can help heal whatever woundings you incurred in childhood (from family or peers), that are (overtly or covertly) undermining your well-being and contributing to your overall stuckness. Rousing will:

- move you toward positive self-regard;
- replace your negative self-talk habits with positive self-talk;
- relieve your overall sense of shame;
- let your unconscious know that you are a good, trustworthy parent to your inner child;
- allow you to experience unconditional love;
- help you feel safer in your daily experiences by (unconsciously) signaling you that you can take care of yourself;
- move you toward personal empowerment through increased self-esteem.

The Mechanics: When using these solutions, you might *see* pictures and images, or have *feelings*, *knowings*, *thoughts*, or alternatively *ideas*. There is no *right* approach.

❖ *Morning Rousing.* For a minimum of one minute (using an egg timer or some other timing device so you won't be distracted by wondering how much time has passed) imagine the child you used to be. Using an actual photograph of yourself (preferably from when you were seven years of age or under) can be helpful at first, but if no photograph is available, simply use your mind's eye to imagine the young "you."

To begin: notice or think about all the exquisite details of yourself as a child. What are you, the child, wearing? What is the expression in your eyes? What could you as a child have been thinking? What was life like when you were a child?

Take your time. When a *clear* picture or idea of yourself as a child forms, begin speaking to yourself with *unconditional* love. Unconditional love is love that has no agenda, or preferences—that's free of focus on behavior, production, or outcome, and that's not defined by the particulars of relationship. It's love without expectation, love that accepts mistakes, personality "flaws," and *all feelings*. Unconditional love statements might include: "I will always be there to support you," "All your feelings are okay with me," "It's all right to make mistakes," "I will listen to your needs," "You deserve my attention," etc.

❖ **On-the-Spot Rousing.** This way of relating to yourself with positive regard will also prove useful in the course of your daily activities. For example, the setting is the boss's office. He's not happy, and as he rattles on and on about your shortcomings, you become anxious, feeling like a kid in trouble. Now, instead of leaning into the anxiety and the internal chaos that anxiety generates, you begin comforting yourself. Even as you're hearing him with one ear, listen to your own inner good-parent voice with the other. Say silently to yourself, "It's okay. Easy does it. Just because I made a mistake doesn't mean I'm bad. Everyone makes mistakes. It's not that big a deal. I believe in you. Relax." Again, the point is to provide *unconditional* loving self-support. This practice can even relieve your immediate anxiety enough to allow you to respond to the boss's complaint without defensiveness!

Solution #3

Meditate

Taking quiet time to explore your inner world.

The Intention: Meditation is a journey to your inner landscape that, over time, helps you map the peaks and valleys, the swamp lands and arid areas inside you, so that you can explore and cross that inner terrain safely and respectfully.

Unfortunately, many people who have never meditated still manage to maintain elaborate and often erroneous opinions about the process. They are likely to think it's a stoic, self-punishing exercise in which the practitioner remains stupidly mindless while sitting in ridiculous, painful

The Fourteen Solutions • 59

positions. In fact, meditation allows the *surface* mind to relax and provides access to the vast wealth of your deep, *unconscious* mind; and you can meditate in almost any position you're able to get into, though some are better than others. Instead of mediation, you might be happier using a more Westernized name, like *purposeful quiet time.*

During mediation, your unconscious may offer you guidance, connection with various sources of wisdom, new ideas, general understanding, specific understanding, long-buried memories, or almost anything else. These things may be presented as *expanded spiritual experiences,* individual *symbols* (the same kinds you see in dreams, and equally rich and challenging to figure out), *complex inner movies, words,* and/or *feelings.* You may receive anything from a rapid parade of incomprehensible mental pictures to a clear sense of *revelation* (inspired realization and/or disclosure). Thus, meditation:

- provides a window to the unconscious;
- clarifies what's happening in your life and offers you direction or inspiration with regard to what you might to do about it all;
- empowers you through that clarity;
- relaxes you and thereby (eventually) creates in your life an overall feeling of increased calm;
- establishes a sense of ritual which, in turn, helps give structure to your life;
- positions you for the surfacing of life-changing revelation;
- teaches you to trust your own inner guidance.

The Mechanics: Start with a simple morning meditation that encourages you to appreciate the day. Many people also find that having wordless, soothing music in the background is helpful.

Begin with the breathing focus suggested in *Solution #1 (Breathe & Center)*. Focus on your breath—relaxing further with each intake. Do not try to *do* anything else. Your purpose is not to develop complicated images or visions, nor is it to go blank. *Whatever* inner events happen while you are focusing are correct. Try doing this for 10 or 15 minutes a day during the next week or so. If doing so feels right, combine your *rousing* time with meditation.

After you find yourself relaxing easily, start introducing additional elements: revisit a recent dream image; focus on a photograph; concentrate on a particular word (anger, love, desire). Afterward, note the feelings, thoughts, and/or *images* that came into your mind. Do this whether or not anything makes sense at the moment. Later, you want to spend a more in-depth period of time with one or more of these feelings or thoughts, but for now simply learn to begin trusting your own inner rhythm, information, and pacing.

Solution #4
Write

Putting your thoughts on paper.

The Intention: Writing is a simple, direct, personal way for you to clearly see the thoughts that filter through your mind and one of the most effective of all tools. Writing stops the random appearance and disappearance of thoughts by compelling you to examine and evaluate them in some kind of logical order. This procedure, which relieves stress as it reveals truth, can be magical and quite often this solution offers nearly instant results. Writing encourages you to:

- express your feelings and, in doing so, start to clarify those feelings;
- understand your own reactivity and the basis for that reactivity;
- reveal your own inner truths *to yourself*;
- stimulate a deeper understanding of the way your own mind works;
- expose your thinking distortions to yourself;
- recognize feelings you didn't even know you have;
- relieve the anxiety that chaotic thinking can produce.

The Mechanics: Aim not for right or wrong answers but for clarity! Whether you're writing in the moment (when something impactful happens) or writing by recall, here's what to do: take pen in hand (or turn on your computer) and become fully present by first breathing in a slow, measured fashion. When the writing begins, be spontaneous. Let whatever comes come. Do not edit. (Note: writing by hand is preferable, as it stimulates the thoughts, feelings, and memories in a different, often more emotionally connected way than do other recording methods. However, if writing by hand is difficult, try the computer. Even a tape recorder will do. Any version of recording your thoughts is better than no version at all.)

Another approach is: enter the exercise with a particular thought, feeling or topic in mind. For example, if you want to consider the effects of anger on your life, start with *Breathe & Center* (Solution #1), and then, while focusing on your breath, think (for example): ANGER, ANGER, ANGER. When you are appropriately moved or motivated, begin to write *without editing*.

"GOOD WHEN LESS IS MORE" SOLUTIONS

Solution #5
Be Here Now

Coming down to earth through mental concentration.

The Intention: Virtually every problem in our lives involves our inability to be and stay in the present time, which manifests either in our being confused and "air-headed" or in our focus on outcomes, eventualities, and potentials. We accept our award before we audition for the play, pick out our china pattern before our first date, demand a raise before the job has started. We worry so much about what *may* or *will* happen that we often miss opportunities staring us right in the face. This solution begins to address this problem by getting you to be aware of *exactly* where you are *now*. Be Here Now:

- brings you down to earth;
- gets you to pay attention to current circumstances and the present time;
- teaches you how to focus;
- allows you to experience enhanced connection with others (and they with you);
- helps improve your concentration, which can, in fact, lead to better outcomes;
- positions you to recognize the gifts of your daily life;
- announces ways in which you may be of service to others.

The Mechanics: *In public:* The next time you're with other people and boredom, distraction, self-involvement, or inattention sets in, try this: become amazingly, outrageously *curious* about the other person. Concentrate. Concentrate. Concentrate. What new information about her can you discover? What have you never noticed before about him that might be of interest? Try repeating silently everything that other person is saying. Also try *echoing* (repeating out loud the essence of what you just heard). This allows the person with whom you are talking to feel heard (because he or she *is* heard—that is, you must <u>know</u> what's been said in order to repeat it). This procedure has the potential of increasing connectedness. Thus, for example, a coworker says, "I'm afraid the boss hates me." Your response: "Why would you think he hates you?"

Perhaps while reading this you're thinking,"What if I don't actually care about that person?" The answer is: "So what?" These solutions are for *your* healing and well-being and you do not have to be in a particular context with others, have a special relationship with them, or even have a definite feeling toward them to practice having a better life.

In private: Of course, not all disconnection occurs in the presence of others. You're perfectly capable of scattering your mental and physical energies when you're alone. This lack of focus makes accomplishment difficult and causes you to miss the pleasure of the moment.

In this case, I recommend an adaptation of an Eastern meditation process. First, find a quiet place, away from other people. Next, close your eyes and focus your breath. Now, start noticing your own specific body sensations. Think, "I feel my right leg against the chair. I feel my left hand on my thigh. I feel the sun on my face." Continue doing this with various parts of your body until you feel *completely* attentive to the present moment.

When a quiet (or solitary) place is unavailable, you can still do this exercise. Here's an example: You're invited to a family function where you and your partner (or date) are going to meet. Right before you leave, the two of you have a fight on the phone. In the car, you start thinking about the fight and anticipating a miserable evening. The more you look ahead, the worse you feel. Mentally, you're building a case for a terrible experience—which may then be what you create out from your anxiety! Instead try to be here now! While still paying careful attention to your driving think: "I feel my right foot on the brake pedal. I feel the steering wheel in my hand. It feels smooth and slightly cold. I feel my butt on the seat of the car." After a time, relaxation and relief will set in, as, the focus switches away from how the evening may go and onto the task at hand—driving the car.

Solution #6
Thought Stop

Interrupting unhealthy thinking.

The Intention: People often imagine that most of their thoughts appear and disappear randomly and even irrationally. This is incorrect. Thoughts are actually *conceived* (although often unconsciously), at what point they can then be given full attention, or they can be ignored or neglected. But when your thoughts are careening out of control (or causing you to careen out of control!), you don't usually feel as though you have any authority over them. During those times you must find a way to override those thoughts. The intention of *Thought stop* is:

- ❀ to offer you freedom from your preoccupations;
- ❀ to provide you (at least) momentary relief from unhealthy thinking;
- ❀ to open the way for new clarity;
- ❀ to increase your productivity through that clarity;
- ❀ to focus your thinking onto the present time and current circumstances;
- ❀ to counter the kind of unproductive thinking that often precedes inappropriate behavior;
- ❀ to allow for the possibility of real connectedness with others and with events.

The Mechanics: Reducing obsessive, aggressive, or negative thinking requires consistency. Considering reality is often a helpful way to begin. This means attempting to see what's *really* going on in your life instead of what you imagine or even wish were going on. Once you've identified the difference between what's real and what is only wishful or fear-driven thinking, you can begin to stop your overactive mind from taking its frantic journeys.

To accomplish this goal, the next time an unwanted thought comes into your head, say to the thought: "Stop!" Say it forcefully, as if you are warning off an unwanted intruder. Say it over and over until the invading thought is gone. Once you have stopped your unhealthy thinking process, it is best to try thinking of something completely different. For instance, an unhealthy relationship of yours has recently ended, and thoughts about your ex keep invading your brain. You want . . . you need to call. You would die to call. You feel like you must, must, *must* pick up that phone. Panic sets in. Now, instead of responding to that desire say "STOP!" to the idea of calling. Say it and say it and say it until you have successfully (at least for the moment) overwhelmed the urge. Try thinking instead about other things. Focus on your great and loving friends, think about the project you're working on, or think about the good things that are in your life right life now.

When you have those urges essentially under control, then you can take another big step, which is to *follow a healthy thought with a healthy action*. Thus, having now decided not to telephone the person you were obsessing over, call someone else, for instance someone to whom you might be of service (helping another person will go a long way in freeing you from *self*-obsession). Or you might call one of those good friends you've been remembering; or actually start working on a project you've been putting off; or *Rouse* by saying, "I'm fine. I'm terrific. I'm really enough! I don't need [a person, a substance, an experience] to feel okay."

You should be aware that your original self-defeating thoughts are likely to return, and you will therefore need to repeat and repeat the *Thought Stop* solution. Not every thought will put up a fight, but many will. Don't be discouraged. As always, persistence is the key to success.

Thought Stop		
Areas where Thought Stopping is most needed	**Current thoughts**	**Best new thoughts**

Solution #7
Contain

Holding back the emotional and/or physical excesses in your life.

The Intention: *Containment* manages the chaos typically connected with the defenses of spilling, compulsion, raging, and gossiping. In doing so, it improves the way you communicate with others. The use of Containment:

- ❀ reduces anxiety—both yours and that of the people with whom you come in contact—by minimizing interior and exterior noise;
- ❀ makes clear communication possible;
- ❀ focuses your attention, which encourages greater productivity;
- ❀ creates an atmosphere wherein other people feel safe to contribute information;
- ❀ tends to make others want to be around you more, which allows for the possibility of greater intimacy;
- ❀ by managing your distracting behavior, permits access to the underlying feelings you have been avoiding through noise. Thus, when others attempt to be more intimate with you, you can now return their efforts by expressing those underlying feelings;
- ❀ gives you more time to see what's really going on in your life and then to fix what's broken.

The Mechanics: To contain: 1) *Breathe*. For sixty seconds, *stop* all physical movement. Inhale . . . exhale . . . inhale . . . 2) *Think* about what you *really* want to say. Breathe. 3) *Decide what comes next*. When you begin to speak again, speak v-e-r-y slowly, taking your time. 4) *Check-in* with your listener(s) to see if what you're saying is really clear and if you are getting your point across. Endeavor to say no more than what might fit on a 3" x 5" card. 5) *Echo*, by repeating the other person's words. Keep it simple. (An example of simple echoing is this: When a friend asks,"Are you going to eat?" you respond, "Yes, I'm going to eat. I'm going at 7 p.m. to that Italian place." Such repetition makes you listen better and also slows you down. 6) *Notice* (and eventually *write* about) the feelings you now realize you previously avoided, the ones that start rising up in the new stillness.

Solution #8
Disengage

Releasing yourself from anything that emotionally ensnares you.

The Intention: The intention of disengagement is to gain freedom from the kinds of entanglements that make you feel sucked in, or forced into somehow explaining, convincing, teaching, responding, or submitting. *Disengagement is not apathy or disinterest.* Rather, it involves a *lack of reactivity,* which means that no matter what your agenda, expectation, inner emotional response, or anticipation of outcome you manage to experience a sense of equilibrium. When you feel misunderstood, unheard, unseen, or powerless, try this solution.

Disengagement can be used in situations of conflict when someone is behaving in a way that seems out of proportion to the circumstances or when you feel "taken hostage" by your own excessive responses. Disengagement:

- brings you a feeling of personal authority in difficult situations;
- allows you to be emotionally present and essentially calm in the face of whatever results come about;
- reduces your reaction to chaos and the disruption that reaction brings;
- creates an inner sense of safety;
- helps you establish and maintain boundaries;
- keeps you from reacting to other people's reactions;
- frees you to identify your own responses, emotions, and notions.

The Mechanics: By using disengagement, you can free yourself in either of two primary ways:

❖ *Disengagement through understanding*: Do that which will clarify the situation in your own mind. The next time a circumstance occurs in which another person's response feels excessive or disproportionate to you, like a battleship in a bathtub, instead of reacting in kind, try saying silently: "This is not about me. This is not about me." Repeat this phrase to yourself over and over, until you understand that most of what happens may *involve* you but it really isn't *about* you! As soon as possible, write about the situation and your response;

❖ ***Disengagement through physical movement***: Do anything that will, even momentarily, break you free from the tension of your connection to the problem. For example, the boss is yelling, and you're feeling ever worse as the moments tick by. You get smaller and smaller. Smaller and *younger*. Escape seems impossible. Try this: Drop something "accidentally" and bend over to pick it up. Or: Mom is on the phone and the conversation is not going well. So, ask Mom to hold on, then put down the phone and breathe three or four times, consciously recognize your disengagement, and return to the call. In any given situation, be creative and devise your own special methods. As soon as you can, move into a *writing* solution and figure out how and why you got so hooked in the first place.

Disengagement		
Areas where disengagement is most needed	**Current behavior**	**Best new action**

"GOOD WHEN MORE IS BETTER" SOLUTIONS

Solution #9
Get it

Taking a fresh, honest look at yourself.

The Intention: *Getting it* means taking <u>complete</u> responsibility for yourself. You can do this by first recognizing that most of your blaming, comparing, judging, criticizing, and obsessing has little or nothing to do with anyone in your life *now*. While *Disengagement* keeps you from getting snagged in the web of others' excessive reactivity, *Get It* keeps you free from your *own* excessive (usually unconscious) *reactivity*. This solution promises to:

- put you in touch with your own thoughts and feelings;
- allow you to see the big picture of your life, by revealing *your* contribution to circumstances;
- position you so you can change those circumstances;
- empower you through clarity;
- illuminate the ways in which you're still stuck in your original story;
- bring you to a recognition of your feeling and thinking themes;
- enhance your communication style.

The Mechanics: Start by looking for some alternatives to your present inner state. To do this you will need to forego the temptation to focus on the horrific deeds that were done *to* you and instead look at *yourself*! For example, ask yourself: "If I weren't thinking about _____ [the mean way Tom talked to me] what would I be *thinking*?" or "If I weren't thinking about _____ [how I never get from Sandy as good as I give!] what would I be *feeling*?" Recording your feelings and/or thoughts with regard to those matters will provide important information. Eventually a pattern is likely to emerge. These patterns are your feeling and thinking *themes*, the blueprints of your thinking and behavior, the blueprints you follow as you recreate situations and relationships.

These (usually three or four) themes are first revealed in your original stories and then repeated time after time, and still are present in your life today. They sound like: *No one ever pays attention to me, I'm always left out, I'm always last on the list of priorities* and are the phrases that reverberate in your head and in your life. It is these repeated themes that ensnare you. When this happens you are once again stuck in your story.

My Feeling/Thinking Themes are:

Theme #1: _____

Theme #2: _____

Theme #3: _____

Solution #10
State the Obvious

Saying out loud exactly what you're thinking in the moment.

The Intention: *State the obvious* is a helpful step if you want to tell the truth and make direct statements, but often find yourself unable to think of the "right" thing to say. It's a way you can, with little risk, step forward rather than retreat or fill an immeasurable gap and rise above an intolerable moment. This solution:

- enhances your communication skills;
- puts you in touch with your own thinking process;
- sets aside the self-consciousness that prevents you from being emotionally present;
- relieves you from momentary anxiety;
- increases your feelings of visibility;
- establishes a greater connection between you and others;
- offers you relief from your obsessive thinking about your fears.

The Mechanics: The way it works is simple—instead of shutting down, speak up; when you feel stuck for something to say, rather than saying nothing, say *exactly* what you are thinking. For example, you're at the funeral of a friend and cannot think of what to say to the family. State the obvious: "I don't know what to say. I can't find the words." Or there's trouble at home, but the complaint is sticking in your throat. Begin with: "This is very hard for me to say. I'm having trouble getting it out." Or you're on a first date—which everyone knows can be difficult. Try saying: "Aren't first dates tough? I always get so nervous."

This procedure, though easy to understand, can be somewhat difficult to put into practice in the beginning. Getting the words out can be hard. A good way to start is: review situations to see how they might have been different; silently notice what you could have said and take notes with regards to your observations and understandings. Eventually you will find yourself able to speak precisely and in the moment.

State the Obvious	
Circumstances	**What I said or did**

Solution #11
Tell the Truth

*Telling other people what you truly think and feel **about yourself**.*

The Intention: If you are pent-up, shut down, confused, or feeling unheard and invisible, *telling the truth* can go far to relieve you. That relief can lead to a complete change in outlook. This solution has a number of exciting results:

- speaking honestly makes you *feel* more trustworthy, because you *are* more trustworthy;
- others see this and start behaving differently toward you. Telling the truth leads to enhanced feelings of self-esteem, which finally leads to new responses from others;
- your own feelings get clearer to *you* as you speak of them;
- you realize that people often haven't understood you because you haven't *made* yourself understood;
- you feel more connected to the people with whom you speak;
- you start to trust that other people *really* understand you;
- the more you practice it, the easier truth-telling becomes.

The Mechanics: Remember that being truthful doesn't mean telling everything you know to everyone you see! *What changes in truth-telling is not the <u>essence</u> of what you're saying, but rather the depth to which you reveal.* That is to say, the better you know and trust the person you're talking to, the more details concerning your feelings you might express. Here is an example of the different levels of truth-telling that might follow the question "How are you today?"

Answer (to grocery clerk):	"Not so good."
Answer (to acquaintance):	"Not so good. I feel overwhelmed by all the changes in my life right now."
Answer (to lover/mate):	"Not so good. I feel much too small and too incompetent to deal with all the responsibility in my life right now. I'm afraid so much of the time."

You will probably find that your first experiments with this kind of truth-telling are best done under impersonal, nonthreatening circumstances, such as with salespersons in stores, tellers in banks, and servers in restaurants. This will help prepare you for the challenges of using truth-telling as part of your intimacy with close friends and family. You are sure to find that this level of honesty brings freshness to every aspect of your life. Honesty invigorates experience.

Tell the Truth		
Situations	**Statements made**	**Real Truths**

Solution #12

Confront

The clear and suitable expression of your moment-to-moment feelings.

The Intention: Over the years, this important form of interaction has acquired a very bad name, largely because it is regarded as an action-of-last-resort, when long-ignored feelings and needs become explosive. Most people therefore think of confrontation as involving conflict or strident, angry demands. This is a limited and negative view that only promotes avoidance. Actually, at best, confrontation is merely a (considerate) truth-telling that is free of any need to control the outcome of the communication! Thus, *Confrontation* has three parts. Part One: *Telling the truth directly.* Part

Two: *Telling that truth with sensitivity.* Part Three: *Letting go of the results of your truth-telling.* Its purpose:

- to preempt potential resentments;
- to stop keeping new secrets that reinforce old stories;
- to increase personal visibility;
- to express your so-called negative feelings in order to avoid the explosion or implosion that is so often the result of repression;
- to express your so-called positive feelings (those that reveal happiness and excitement) and thereby add to your sense of well-being and interpersonal connection;
- to recognize and validate the importance of your own truth;
- to promote authenticity and the intimacy that comes from that authenticity.

The Mechanics: The temptation is to misunderstand this solution by taking it as permission to give voice to whatever pops into your head. This is absolutely *not* the point, since it omits the proviso about being sensitive. Further, confrontation is not, nor has it ever been, about what *other* people are doing wrong. Rather, it is about what *you* are feeling, thinking, and experiencing. Its aim is for you to talk forthrightly *about yourself.* In order to do this, you must clarify your own needs and wants *before* you speak. Only then can you attempt to articulate these needs and wants effectively and directly to others.

Remember that, generally, when you're talking about your feelings, the word that describes the feeling will directly follow the words "I feel." For example: "I feel sad," "I feel lusty," "I feel rejected," or "I feel exhilarated." However, when you follow the words "I feel" with "that" or "like," you're usually about to launch into a diatribe about the *other* person. For example: "I feel *that* you are a jerk" or "I feel *like* you are sabotaging me," in contrast to "I feel railroaded," or "I feel sabotaged."

Whether or not a *Confrontation* is appropriate depends both on the *nature of the statement* being made (its importance, immediacy, and/or emotional content) and on the *character of the relationship* (depth of connection) that is involved. *Confrontations* are most appropriate whenever *not* expressing something will injure a relationship—to another person or to yourself. If the confrontive statement is difficult for you and the individual toward whom it is directed is important to you, choosing a private place and unhurried time is likely to be best.

You might gain experience with the confrontation process by telling someone how much you appreciate him/her. Watch what happens. Notice his or her feelings before, during, and after the confrontation. Practice at this (positive) level for a while, then be brave enough to choose a disappointment or regret to communicate. Again, notice the other person's feelings before, during, and after. Repeat this process with several different kinds of people—intimates, coworkers, acquaintances, strangers, powerful people, people you feel are less powerful than you. Continue to examine and evaluate the responses—yours as well as others'—to what you say.

Confrontation			
Person Confronted	**Statements made**	**Their response** (words or actions)	**My response** (inside and out)

"GOOD WHEN ACTION IS NEEDED" SOLUTIONS

Solution #13
Take Contrary Action

Doing the opposite of what you have been doing.

The Intention: Insanity has been defined as "behaving the same way over and over again and expecting to get different results." And you know it's true. Eating the same bad food keeps you fat . . . dating the same unavailable partner keeps you lonely . . . and staying at the same unstimulating job keeps you bored. Therefore, if what you're doing is not working, you need to *Take Contrary Action* and change the way you approach both your life and your relationships on a daily basis.

This tool, if applied rigorously, changes your life immediately! For it *not* to do so is impossible. Moreover, changing your actions leads to changes in your attitude, and that will lead to changes in *you*. This solution:

- offers *instant change*. Instant change gives you instant encouragement, which promotes further change;
- illuminates current behaviors;
- shifts your negative habits;
- teaches you how to establish and maintain boundaries;
- establishes clarity in place of confusion;
- causes you to appreciate your own abilities;
- changes your relationships with others.

The Mechanics: First, recognize the way you now think, feel and behave (refer to your most often used defenses and the way they usually work in your life). Begin by making a list of the things that *do not* work in your life (friendships, weight, job). Then, beside each item, note your current behavior in regard to that item.

Complaint	Current Behavior
"I don't have enough friends."	"I seldom call anyone." "I don't return calls promptly." "I rarely ask for help." "I keep my problems to myself."

After you've formed a clear picture of what you're doing now, you're ready to consider the contrary action you can take. List each of them.

Complaint	Current Behavior	New Behavior
"I don't have enough friends."	"I seldom call anyone." "I don't return calls promptly." "I rarely ask for help." "I keep my problems to myself."	Call more often Return calls promptly Reach out Share concerns
Your Complaint	*Your Current Behavior*	*Your New Behavior*

Solution #14
Get Moving

Adding new emotionally and/or physically healthy activity to your daily life.

The Intention: Habitually feeling stuck or powerless may have left you with a sense of helplessness and a belief that you're unable to accomplish anything meaningful or lasting. But both stuckness and powerlessness are *notions* rather than realities. In either case, action is often the best antidote. This solution:

- ❈ creates immediate and tangible change in your life;
- ❈ provides an instant sense of accomplishment, while encouraging you to go forward toward even more change. You not only feel good today, but you also establish habits that prepare you to feel good tomorrow;
- ❈ stimulates new thinking;
- ❈ encourages you to recognize how extensive your creative and energetic resources are;
- ❈ builds self-esteem through positive reinforcement;
- ❈ allows you to begin feeling more powerful about your life;
- ❈ changes the way other people perceive you and therefore the way they behave toward you.

The Mechanics: Begin by noticing where you feel least effective and least fulfilled. Create a list of changes you could make and actions you could take in those areas. Be realistic, though. Only list tasks that are actually feasible.

Now, very, very s-l-o-w-l-y, *Get Moving* and begin chipping away at the list. For example: "I don't exercise"—change that to *five minutes of exercise every other day*. "I don't socialize"—change that to *coffee with another person once a week*. "I frequently complain about the way other people behave"—change that to *once a week compliment or express gratitude*.

Get Moving		
Areas of needed change	**Potential reactions**	**Accomplished actions**

CHAPTER 3

THE DEFENSE ALTERNATIVES

Alternate routes

You are well along in your journey of discovery. You know which defenses you use most often and what kinds of situations or people stimulate those defenses. And you have examined the *fourteen solutions*, the conscious actions that can help you change your usual responses and perhaps even your old attitudes.

This chapter indicates specific solutions for particular defenses. These combinations are the ones my experience has shown me to be most effective—but they are only suggestions. Find out through *your* own efforts which solutions work best for you.

HOW THE DEFENSE ALTERNATIVES WORK

Over and over again you will be asked to confront your fears. Only by doing so can you begin to diminish and finally eliminate the power these defenses hold over you. Thus:

Workout #2

Go toward, go toward, go toward. Face your fears and invite lasting change.

Your fears boil down to one of two fundamental concerns. The first (and most common) is your fear of *being seen*—seen for who you *really* are or, more particularly, for (the incapable, worth-less, unsavory person) you see yourself to be. It is that distorted self-view that encourages your involvement with abandonment, rejection, and ridicule.

The second concerns your fear of *being unseen*. You believe that neither your true self nor your talents will ever be recognized. Again, this fear often drives you to expect abandonment, rejection and ridicule.

The following section offers a thumbnail sketch in the case of each defense that includes:

Most likely underlying problems: This is a brief phrase that attempts to pinpoint the particular fear that most likely provokes each defense.

Intention of alternatives: This sets forth the two-part aim of the alternative behaviors.

Defense Express Ways: This section lists various behaviors and attitudes that ordinarily express the defense in your life. (Circle the words that apply most to you. Also, add your own words.)

Alternate Routes: This alerts you to new potential behaviors. Included in each is a **starred defense** [marked with a "☆"]—the particular alternative behavior that, among the four suggested options, is the one I have observed to be *most* helpful. If you're only going to make one stab at altering your defensive habits, try the starred defense.*

My Personal Discoveries: At the end of each section, you will find space to write about your own experience with alternate routes. As always, if other alternatives that are not listed

---

* Please note that the following list of defenses and their recommended alternatives does not include specific references to either Solution #1 (Rouse) or to Solution #2 (Meditate). This is because both of these Solutions can and probably should be included in a daily routine for building and maintaining healthy self-esteem. The sooner you start this daily regimen the better.

work better for you, use those instead. And of course, *do not* be confined by the limited space offered herein.

In addition, many of the alternatives within each listed defense include recommended journaling or record-keeping suggestions (such as, make a list of new actions to take, little by little take those actions, and record the feelings that come up after doing something new). It is helpful to have a special book earmarked exclusively for this particular purpose. Get one you can easily carry with you (in a purse, briefcase, or pocket).

HIT DEFENSES: CONNECTION THROUGH FEELING

The defense of ANGER
Protecting yourself with feelings of hostility.

Most likely underlying problem: Fear of expressing feelings directly.
Intention of alternatives: ◊ To be free from emotional reactivity; ◊ To gain practice with direct expression.

ANGER EXPRESS WAYS

- indignation
- provoking
- swearing
- sarcasm

- bullying
- arrogance
- shouting
- violence

- rage
- teasing
- sulking
- hostility

- irritability
- bitterness
- retaliating
- insulting

ALTERNATE ROUTES

Write about grief and fear. Be as specific and detailed as possible. How were these feelings expressed in your family when you were growing up? What kinds of things now make you most sad? When do you feel fear?

_____

_____

_____

☆**Breathe & Center**. Consciously regulated breathing can gentle the angry giant. For just a moment, stop all physical movement and breathe into your heart (see p. 56). Now, slowly count to 20. Think about what you would be feeling if you were not lashing out ("I would feel powerless [hurt, unheard, ignored]").

Disengage. Sometimes you just need to remove yourself physically from proximity to the apparent source of your anger (leave the room, hang up the phone). Stay separate from that which has seemed to trigger you until you can determine—through contemplation, writing, or discussion with others—the true origins of your reaction (usually something in your own history).

State the Obvious. Instead of letting anger command your tone, attitude, and behavior, try putting your feelings into exact words. This containment and clarity will benefit both you and those around you with whom you feel the anger. If you do not know what particular words to use, just say, "I'm so angry right now I could scream [cry, blow up, throw dishes, slap you across the room, rip your heart out]." Of course, the companion notion is that instead of *acting* in accord with your feelings, you *speak* of those feelings. You do not throw dishes, slap someone across the room, or rip anyone's heart out. The intention is to express yourself without doing physical or emotional damage that you will regret later.

My Personal Discoveries

My favorite alternative to Anger is: _____

An example of the way I've used this alternative is: _____

_____

The result has been: _____

_____

_____

HIT DEFENSES: CONNECTION THROUGH FEELING

The defense of CONTEMPT FOR OTHERS
Protecting yourself with despising, negative, disdainful feelings toward other people.

Most likely underlying problem: Fear that you, yourself, are worthy of contempt.
Intention of alternatives: ◊ To stop your expression of contempt toward others; ◊ To confront your self-contempt.

CONTEMPT FOR OTHERS EXPRESS WAYS

• judgment	• aggression	• arrogance	• disdain
• cutting humor	• ridicule	• stridency	• self-righteousness
• silence	• despising	• disrespect	• mocking
• separation	• negativity	• swearing	• rejecting

ALTERNATE ROUTES

☆ ***Write*** about (make a list) of all the things you hope others do not notice about you. When, where, and with whom are these characteristics most likely to surface? When did you first start to dislike these traits? What do you think will happen if others do notice them?

_____

_____

_____

Thought Stop. The idea is to block the derogatory, disparaging notions and the endless mental criticism. In their place, substitute thoughts of gratitude and appreciation (instead of focusing on how stupid the people you work with are, notice the benefits you derive from your work with them; rather than making a list of the things your spouse forgot to do, realize what's been accomplished; and, in general, instead of emphasizing what you dislike about life, focus on what's good). Gratitude lists work well here.

Contain. As your awareness grows, follow your healthier thinking with healthy behavior. Refrain from gossip, criticism, mocking, ridicule, and judgment. List* the feelings and/or thoughts you have when you're not slurring others.

Take Contrary Action. Your aggression towards others often leaves you feeling separate and alone. Find ways to connect. Notice what's likable about other people or what you have in common.

My Personal Discoveries

My favorite alternative to Contempt for Others is: _____

An example of the way I've used this alternative is: _____
_____

The result has been: _____
_____
_____

HIT DEFENSES: CONNECTION THROUGH FEELING

The defense of BLAME

Protecting yourself by feeling and believing that someone else is at fault.

Most likely underlying problem: Fear of having no real authority over your own life.
Intention of alternatives: ◊ To stop the blame; ◊ To encourage empowerment via accountability.

BLAME EXPRESS WAYS

- resentment
- deflecting focus
- accusation
- excuse-making
- complaint
- criticism
- self-righteousness
- gossiping
- outrage
- reproach
- whining
- paralysis
- denunciation

* *Listing* is a shorthand way to look at your behavior. It can be done quickly and without any in-depth probing.

ALTERNATE ROUTES

Write about the way authority was exhibited in your household when you were growing up. How did you feel about that exhibition, and how did you respond?

_____

_____

_____

Contain. The more blame you practice, the more at the mercy of other people you will feel. Cut out the negative talk, eye-rolling, disdainful noises, reproach, complaining, and denunciation.

Get It. Stop wasting so much mental energy pointing the finger at others. Instead ruminate and journal about what *you do* to contribute to the problems in your life (choose badly, ignore the signs, hesitate to speak your mind).

☆*Tell the Truth*. Begin expressing your fears. Speak of the paralysis, disappointment, reluctance, and self-doubt you have. Whatever you think about others, turn it around and say it about yourself ("She never takes my feelings into account" becomes "I never take her feelings into account" or "I neglect myself").

My Personal Discoveries

My favorite alternative to Blame is: _____

An example of the way I've used this alternative is: _____

_____

The result has been: _____

_____

_____

HIT DEFENSES: CONNECTION THROUGH DOING

The defense of SPILLING

Protecting yourself with constant (often inappropriate) talking.

Most likely underlying problem: Fear of loneliness.
Intention of alternatives: ◊ To learn containment; ◊ To practice connection.

SPILLING EXPRESS WAYS

- gossiping
- babbling
- repetition
- flamboyance
- loud talk
- declamations
- boundarilessness
- inappropriate behavior

ALTERNATE ROUTES

Write about where and when you learned to drown out your feelings with noise? What feelings do you suspect you are most afraid of? Why?

_____
_____
_____

Breathe & Center. The breathless spiller talks first and thinks later. So stop . . . take several breaths. Think about *why* you are talking and what you *really* want to say.

☆*Contain.* Hold back your babble by: (1) Speaking in a precise manner; (2) Thinking before you speak; (3) Communicating simple thoughts; and (4) Saying only as much as might fit on a 3x5 card.

Tell the Truth. What happens when the exterior and interior noise stops. Be direct and thorough in telling others about the discoveries you've made about yourself. Then list your reactions to this experience of exposure.

My Personal Discoveries

My favorite alternative to Spilling is: _____

An example of the way I've used this alternative is: _____

_____

The result has been: _____

_____

_____

HIT DEFENSES: CONNECTION THROUGH DOING

The defense of GOSSIP

Protecting yourself by talking to someone about someone else who is not present.

Most likely underlying problem: Fear of revelatory self-disclosure.
Intention of alternatives: ◇ To stop the gossip; ◇ To encourage self-disclosure.

GOSSIP EXPRESS WAYS

• judgment	• negativity	• comparing	• spreading rumors
• contempt	• ridicule	• creating scandal	• superiority
• covert behavior	• no boundaries	• whispering	• shaming
• rejection	• disdain	• self-righteousness	• arrogance

ALTERNATE ROUTES

Write about your fear of *self*-disclosure. When are you most intimidated, shut down, or hesitant. What's going to happen if people really get to know who you are inside?

_____

_____

_____

☆***Contain***. Stop dishing the dish, spreading the news, relaying messages, playing the middleman, making snide comments, and judging the actions of others. As usual, notice what feelings arise in you when you cease your usual behavior.

Disengage. It's easy to get entangled in the gossip net—especially if you're known as someone who likes gossip. Pull away from such conversations, then notice (and notate) what you feel.

Confront. Talking about other people is a common distraction from self-revelation. Connect in different, creative ways (especially to your usual gossip partner). Ask, for instance, about his/her life and volunteer information about your own life. Talk about *your* feelings rather than someone else's behavior. Now that you're becoming more intimate, start talking about things you would ordinarily hesitate to speak of.

My Personal Discoveries

My favorite alternative to Gossip is: _____

An example of the way I've used this alternative is: _____

The result has been: _____

HIT DEFENSES: CONNECTION THROUGH DOING

The defense of HUMOR

Protecting yourself with comical (sometimes inappropriate) self-expression.

Most likely underlying problem: Fear of vulnerability.
Intention of alternatives: ◊ To gain authority over when and where you express your humor; ◊ To promote healthy vulnerability.

HUMOR EXPRESS WAYS

- flippancy
- attack
- teasing
- ridicule
- provoking
- negativity
- sarcasm
- disdain

ALTERNATE ROUTES

Write about the "serious" side of life. What topics are you most hesitant to look at in depth (death, love, sexuality, God, aging)? Pick one and write about it.

_____

_____

_____

Breathe & Center. Humor often begins with a rush of snappy thoughts. Start by focusing on your breath instead of your witty repartee.

Contain. Humor can be a slap in the face and a push away. Cease and desist. Hold back the quips, barbs, jests, sarcastic remarks, and ridicule. Notice what you feel when you're not poking fun.

☆***Take Contrary Action.*** Once you've stopped the negative "expressions" of humor, try something new. (1) Instead of pushing away—move toward others (compliment the very individual you're tempted to tease); (2) rather than provoking—evoke (instead of thinking something negative, become interested and ask a question); (3) instead of attacking—share (don't tell others what's wrong with them, talk about your own concerns). Jot down your responses following each new action.

My Personal Discoveries

My favorite alternative to defensive Humor is: _____

An example of the way I've used this alternative is: _____

_____

The result has been: _____

_____

_____

HIT DEFENSES: CONNECTION THROUGH DOING

The defense of DEPENDENCE
Protecting yourself through excessive reliance on others.

Most likely underlying problem: Fear of attempting to realize your own capacity.
Intention of alternatives: ◇ To move toward independence; ◇ To begin to recognize your areas of real capacity.

DEPENDENCE EXPRESS WAYS

- fearfulness
- insecurity
- reliance
- victim posture

- complaint
- procrastination
- incomplete tasks
- indirectness

- confusion
- disorganization
- jealousy
- manipulation

- submissiveness
- paralysis
- self-centeredness
- lethargy

ALTERNATE ROUTES

Write about the most powerful person(s) in your family of origin (what they were like, how they treated you when you were growing up, and what they taught you—either through communication or by example—about power and success). What do you tell yourself about your own potential power and success in any area?

_____
_____
_____

Get It. Begin discovering and investigating the thematic ideas that are keeping you stuck. What are your (internal) complaints about the difficulties in your life?

Confront. You already have much more information than you realize about almost everything. Make a long list of all your beliefs, opinions, and attitudes. Now when you're with other people, start speaking *directly* about these things . . . even when doing so threatens to rock the safety boat.

☆***Get Moving.*** "I've always depended on the kindness of strangers," says classic dependent Blanche DuBois in Tennessee Williams' drama *A Streetcar Named Desire*. Like most dependents,

Blanche is all about show and little about go. Confront your own tendency to wait for someone else to fix your life. Make a list of the areas in your life where you're least effective and then attempt slowly but surely to change your behavior in those areas: begin to get organized; finish *one* project; make lists of what needs to be done; and do things without asking advice.

My Personal Discoveries

My favorite alternative to Dependence is: _____

An example of the way I've used this alternative is: _____

_____

The result has been: _____

_____

_____

HIT DEFENSES: CONNECTION THROUGH DOING

The defense of CODEPENDENCE

Protecting yourself through excessive reliance on people or things to define your self-worth.

Most likely underlying problem: Fear of worthlessness.
Intention of alternatives: ◇ To contain your codependent behavior; ◇ To build self-esteem through visibility.

CODEPENDENCE EXPRESS WAYS

• excessive diligence	• controlling behavior	• people-pleasing	• approval-seeking
• overworking	• feeling burdened	• boundarilessness	• excessive worry
• compliance	• caretaking	• overwhelm	• excessive activity
• resentment	• perfectionism		

ALTERNATE ROUTES

☆ *Write* about your worthwhileness in terms of the following topics: Define self-worth. What behavior was valued most in your house when you were growing up? What do *you* like most about yourself now?

_____
_____
_____

Contain. The first step is to stop being so helpful. Remember, your helpfulness is in large part an effort to control what other people think of you. Stop advising, assisting, and doing everything yourself. Notice your feelings in the face of this cessation of activity.

Get It. When do you remember first deciding to be a caretaker? What value do you think this behavior still has for you now?

Tell the Truth. You people-please, engage in excessive activity, and try to regulate how others perceive you. Try to understand the function of these behaviors in your life, then share with others about what you learn.

My Personal Discoveries

My favorite alternative to Codependence is: _____

An example of the way I've used this alternative is: _____
_____

The result has been: _____
_____
_____

HIT DEFENSES: CONNECTION THROUGH DOING

The defense of THERAPIZING

Protecting yourself through excessive (often unrequested) advice-giving.

Most likely underlying problem: Fear of experiencing and expressing feelings.
Intention of alternatives: ◇ To stop the therapizing; ◇ To put you in touch with your feelings.

THERAPIZING EXPRESS WAYS

- advising
- controlling
- instruction
- intrusion
- boundarilessness
- constant analysis
- righteousness
- lecturing
- ignoring feelings
- arrogance
- insistent attitude
- constant solutions

ALTERNATE ROUTES

Write about spontaneity and intuition. As a child, what were you taught about these two things? What do you think would happen if you lived as much (or even more) by feelings as by thought?

_____
_____
_____

☆***Breathe & Center.*** You are trapped in your head. To escape that trap, focus by breathing slowly and deliberately. Pay attention to your *feeling* responses to other people. Where in your body do those responses occur? Characterize those responses.

Contain. When you feel tempted leap into another person's web of troubles and you want to "help," first *stop*, *breathe*, and *wait*! Notice what happens.

State the Obvious. When you feel like "helping" by analyzing, advising, lecturing, or instructing, try instead to notice your own *feelings*. Once you've recognized those feelings, speak up about them.

My Personal Discoveries

My favorite alternative to Therapizing is: _____

An example of the way I've used this alternative is: _____
_____

The result has been: _____
_____
_____

HIT DEFENSES: CONNECTION THROUGH DOING

The defense of CONTROL
Protecting yourself by exercising a regulating or directing influence.

Most likely underlying problem: Fear of being out of control.
Intention of alternatives: ◇ To stop the controlling behavior; ◇ To discover that things don't fall apart when you relax your control.

CONTROL EXPRESS WAYS

• focus on outcome	• superiority	• emotionlessness	• bossiness
• arrogance	• repression	• self-righteousness	• criticism
• hyper-organization	• coercing behavior	• hypervigilance	• perfectionism
• dominion	• uptightness	• constant instruction	• authoritativeness

ALTERNATE ROUTES

☆ *Write* about the chaos in your house when you were growing up. Describe it in detail. How did that chaos make you feel and what did you do in the face of those feelings?

_____

_____

_____

Tell the Truth. Understanding is only half the battle. Now find someone with whom to share your discoveries. Notice (and afterward notate) your feelings during that kind of sharing.

Get It. Stop white-knuckling your way through life. Find out why you're holding on so tight. Make a list of reasons why you might be afraid of letting go.

Take Contrary Action. (1) Try expressing your *own* feelings rather than worrying about what others should do, feel, or think; (2) Stop instructing and contribute instead (include others by inviting them to add their own information to the mix); (3) You're burdened by worry about how everything will turn out. Focus instead on what's happening right now.

My Personal Discoveries

My favorite alternative to Control is: _____

An example of the way I've used this alternative is: _____

_____

*The result has been:*_____

_____

_____

HIT DEFENSES: CONNECTION THROUGH DOING

The defense of CRITICISM
Protecting yourself by constantly finding fault

Most likely underlying problem: Fear of failure.
Intention of alternatives: ◇ To stop criticizing; ◇ To learn appreciation.

CRITICISM EXPRESS WAYS

• negativity	• judgment	• disappointment	• perfectionism
• rejection	• cynicism	• blame	• impatience
• ridicule	• condemnation	• contempt	• insistence

ALTERNATE ROUTES

Write about your disappointments. Go back as far as you can, noting what you were taught about how to handle such frustrations. What things disappoint you now and what do you do about your disappointment?

_____
_____
_____

☆*Thought Stop*. Drain your brain of negative thoughts. Try substituting another line of thinking. Thus, for example, instead of focusing on what you dislike about others, consider what you appreciate about them.

Tell the Truth. Face your interior discomfort. Share with those closest to you what you've learned about the critical inner voice in your life (who at home was most critical when you were growing up? What happened then when mistakes were made? What happens inside you now when you fall short of the mark?). *Exactly* what do you criticize yourself about? Write, write, write.

Take Contrary Action. (1) Rather than indulging in contempt, find ways to compliment; (2) instead of rejecting, approach; (2) rather than focusing on failure, notice what works; instead of finding what's missing, discover the value of what you have.

My Personal Discoveries

My favorite alternative to Criticism is: _____

An example of the way I've used this alternative is: _____
_____

The result has been: _____
_____
_____

HIT DEFENSES: CONNECTION THROUGH THINKING

The defense of PROJECTION

Protecting yourself by using other people as a screen for unconscious thoughts and feelings.

Most likely underlying problem: Fear of self-awareness.
Intention of alternatives: ◊ To pave the way for understanding your own unconscious; ◊ To release you from the vast limitations that this defense creates.

PROJECTION EXPRESS WAYS

- assumptiveness
- blame
- fantasy

- unconsciousness
- denial
- comparing

- judgment
- prejudice
- self-centeredness

- hypervigilance
- paranoia
- self-consciousness

ALTERNATE ROUTES

Write a brief description of your own personality characteristics (the traits that cumulatively define you). Use one-word or two-word identifiers, such as "athletic" or "cheap."

_____

_____

_____

☆*Get It*. "Mirror, mirror on the wall—is anything I see true . . . at all?" Start by assuming that everything you believe others are thinking or feeling (but that they've not actually said) about *you* is, in fact, your idea of *yourself* ("She doesn't like me" becomes "I don't like me"). Now, also consider that these thoughts may be *your* idea of those others ("I don't like her"). Keep a daily notebook that thoroughly documents these reversals.

Confront. Now that you've begun to recognize and track your thinking, reveal to others what you *imagine* they think about you and find out what they are *actually* thinking or intending.

Take Contrary Action. Do the opposite of what you've been doing. That is, (1) rather than rejecting someone you're convinced dislikes you, figure out what *you like* about him/her; (2) when you're tempted to bail on a circumstance because you think no one wants you there, notice what you have to contribute, and then make that contribution.

My Personal Discoveries

My favorite alternative to Projection is: _____

An example of the way I've used this alternative is: _____

_____

The result has been: _____

_____

_____

Defense Alternatives • 99

HIT DEFENSES: CONNECTION THROUGH THINKING

The defense of JUDGMENT
Protecting yourself with opinions that tend to be moral, critical, or righteous.

Most likely underlying problem: Fear of being judged.
Intention of alternatives: ◇ To stop the judgment; ◇ To discover the source of this defense.

JUDGMENT EXPRESS WAYS

- inflexibility
- righteousness
- criticizing
- comparing
- inappropriateness
- didacticism
- unapproachability
- attack
- rigidity
- rule-giving
- rejection
- strident opinion-giving
- superiority
- controlling behavior
- contempt

ALTERNATE ROUTES

Write about the ways in which you felt judged when you were growing up. How do you think these judgments affected your self-esteem?

_____
_____
_____

Thought Stop. Judgment interrupts relationships the way call-waiting interrupts telephone calls. Therefore, block the intrusive thoughts—the interrupting beeps—and instead focus completely on the person with whom you are speaking. What really interests you about him? What can you do (right now!) to feel closer to her?

Tell the Truth. When you are with other people, silently wonder to yourself, "If I weren't judging your beauty [intelligence, earning capacity, sexual openness, social grace] what would I be feeling about *myself* in this regard?" Write about these feelings.

☆*Get Moving*. Judgment leaves little time for playful, loving interaction or personal expansion. Instead: (1) Spend a day gathering new information from others without contributing your opinions about what they are saying; (2) Read a book that offers a completely new perspective—

perhaps even something with which you now disagree; (3) Go somewhere you never go. Try these three suggestions and notice how you feel while enacting them.

My Personal Discoveries

My favorite alternative to Judgment is: _____

An example of the way I've used this alternative is: _____
_____

The result has been: _____
_____
_____

HIT DEFENSES: CONNECTION THROUGH THINKING

The defense of COMPARING

Protecting yourself by measuring the way you feel against the way others appear.

Most likely underlying problem: Fear of intimacy.
Intention of alternatives: ◊ To stop comparing; ◊ To practice intimacy.

COMPARING EXPRESS WAYS

- judgment
- criticism
- withdrawal
- contrasting
- vigilance
- disdain
- rejection
- self-contempt
- other-contempt

ALTERNATE ROUTES

Write about keeping up with the Joneses. Suppose others *do* have more than you . . . so what? What will happen if you fall behind? When you were growing up, how did your parents talk about other people?

_____

_____

_____

Thought Stop. Stop thinking about how you measure up. When tempted to compare yourself with others, focus on the similarities instead of the differences.

☆*Confront*. How people *look* to you seldom describes the way those people *feel* inside. Check out your assumptions. Ask people direct questions about their experience and be willing to believe what they tell you.

Get Moving. Make a list of things that actually need to change if you're to have a better life (get exercise, go back to school, enlarge your circle of friends). Begin to go after what you want.

My Personal Discoveries

My favorite alternative to Comparing is: _____

An example of the way I've used this alternative is: _____

_____

The result has been: _____

_____

_____

HIT DEFENSES: CONNECTION THROUGH THINKING

The defense of ANALYZING

*Protecting yourself through intellectual examination
that discounts emotional or intuitive factors.*

Most likely underlying problem: Fear of feeling.
Intention of alternatives: ◊ To stop the analysis; ◊ To learn how to access your feelings.

ANALYZING EXPRESS WAYS

• investigation	• intrusion	• dismissiveness	• passionlessness
• rationalization	• scrutiny	• criticism	• control
• skepticism	• dissection	• therapizing	• didacticism

ALTERNATE ROUTES

☆ ***Write*** about the first time you realized that feeling "too much" was a bad idea. When you were a child, how were feelings treated and greeted in your family? When you were growing up, who did you talk to about those feelings?

_____
_____
_____

Breathe & Center. Start moving out of your head by breathing into your body. With each breath, picture your thoughts dissolving and being replaced with feelings. What feelings are they?

Get It. The logical mind can be a proficient instrument for exploring obscure or unknown regions of your psyche, including places where old wounds are kept out of sight. Use this investigatory ability to delve into less familiar aspects of your sadness, madness, and gladness. Notate what do you when these feelings arise. Find someone you trust and tell him/her some of your hidden or worrisome truths. Write about what you feel after the conversation.

Take Contrary Action. The analyzer minimizes feelings. Therefore, sound off less with your (heady) words, while expressing your emotions more! When you are tempted to figure things out—wonder about your own feeling-state instead; stop dismissing feelings (yours and other people's). Instead, acknowledge and accept them. Rather than controlling, cooperate.

My Personal Discoveries

My favorite alternative to Analyzing is: _____

An example of the way I've used this alternative is: _____
_____

The result has been: _____
_____
_____

HIT DEFENSES: CONNECTION THROUGH THINKING

The defense of MASKING
Protecting yourself by saying one thing while feeling or thinking another.

Most likely underlying problem: Fear of rejection.
Intention of alternatives: ◊ To stop hiding and move toward visibility; ◊ To face your fear.

MASKING EXPRESS WAYS

- hiding
- secretiveness
- lying
- contempt
- people-pleasing
- minimizing
- rejecting
- inauthenticity
- editing
- compliance
- artifice
- bravado

ALTERNATE ROUTES

Write about what you think will happen if people really get to know you. When did you begin to develop the art of hiding out? What happened to inspire that development?
_____
_____
_____

Be Here Now. Masking inevitably involves your worry about the future—about what's *going* to happen (what will others think and how will it all turn out?). Begin by becoming present and learning how to pay attention to exactly what's happening in front of you *now*.

Tell the Truth. Most people are not in the habit of expressing themselves with candor. That's probably true of you, also. Therefore, slowly but surely start revealing more of yourself to others, especially the so-called negative emotions of the moment. At first, choose the easiest people to tell (in dialogue with curious grocery clerk: Q: "How are you today?" A: "Grumpy").

☆ ***Confront.*** Maskers are circuitous—fearing that truth will bring unwanted consequences. There's only one way to confront this erroneous idea and that is to say what you mean and mean what you say. Begin by keeping a daily diary. For one week merely note what you would *like* to say but do *not* say (focus at first on "positive" unspoken expressions, like "I love the way you move your hands when you talk" or "I appreciate your help"). Then spend the next week actually revealing these kinds of things to others (and writing in your notebook about the experiences). Now, spend one week recording your so-called "negative" responses, and another week revealing these responses ("I feel overwhelmed" or "When you snap at me I want to leave"). Pay close attention to the results in both instances. Again, record the experience.

My Personal Discoveries

My favorite alternative to Masking is: _____

An example of the way I've used this alternative is: _____
_____

The result has been: _____
_____
_____

RUN DEFENSES: DISCONNECTION THROUGH FEELING

The defense of SHAME

Protecting yourself through your all-pervasive sense of basic defectiveness.

Most likely underlying problem: Fear that something is really wrong with you.
Intention of alternatives: ◊ To stop the shame; ◊ To get comfortable with having personal power.

SHAME EXPRESS WAYS

- disrespect
- superiority
- blame
- paranoia
- righteousness
- ridicule
- embarrassment
- rejection
- arrogance
- degradation
- negativity
- self-contempt
- secretiveness
- self-abuse
- other-abuse

ALTERNATE ROUTES

Write about your first realizations that something seemed wrong with you. Where did you get this idea? What happened to confirm your self-doubt? When you were growing up, what messages did you receive about self-esteem?

_____
_____
_____

Get It. Figure out how you're shaming yourself and other people. Keep a daily record of things you do and say to yourself and others that are shaming. Be specific. If indirect complaint is one of your methods of shaming, try instead to clearly tell others how you really feel.

☆*Contain*. Whether your problem is being shamed or shaming other people, the initial cure is the same—to establish boundaries. First, stop saying rude things to yourself. Second, stop the shaming remarks or looks that send shaming messages to others.

Get Moving. Nothing changes things like change! Create a list of activities that enhance your self-esteem (that make you feel good about your life, such as: exercising, treating yourself to a special event, meeting with friends, snuggling with your cat). Now, do one of those things every few days. Record how you feel afterward.

My Personal Discoveries

My favorite alternative to Shame is: _____

An example of the way I've used this alternative is: _____
_____

The result has been: _____

_____

_____

RUN DEFENSES: DISCONNECTION THROUGH FEELING

The defense of SELF-CONTEMPT

Protecting yourself by using excessive expressions of self-disdain.

Most likely underlying problem: Fear of high self-esteem.
Intention of alternatives: ◇ To stop the self-contempt; ◇ To invite positive self-esteem.

SELF-CONTEMPT EXPRESS WAYS

- complaint
- negativity
- secretiveness
- self-derision
- mocking
- rejecting
- helplessness
- self-sabotage
- comparing

ALTERNATE ROUTES

Write a list indicating the ways in which you are incredible, accomplished, inspirational, terrific, exciting, etc. Do this as if no one else will ever see (or judge) what you are writing. Be expansive. Read this list to yourself out loud daily for 30 days.

_____

_____

_____

☆*Thought Stop.* Interrupt and replace your self-detesting inner dialogue either with self-investigatory questions ("If I weren't beating up on myself, what would I be thinking or feeling?") or with questions that can lead to alternative behaviors ("What do I need to do right now to feel better/stronger/more powerful?") As always, it's best to follow understanding with action.

Get It. Discover and admit to yourself the advantages of holding on to self-contempt (you don't have to expect much of yourself, you can assume you will disappoint others so you can pull your punch in relationships, you can fail without blaming yourself too harshly). Now disclose and expose your discoveries to at least one other person.

Contain. Self-contempt reflects old, unrelieved sore spots. Go back as far as you can in your memory to recall and list the major resentments of your life. Keep each item to 3-4 words. Notice how these old resentments find their way into your current relationships.

My Personal Discoveries

My favorite alternative to Self-Contempt is: _____

An example of the way I've used this alternative is: _____
_____

The result has been: _____
_____
_____

RUN DEFENSES: DISCONNECTION THROUGH FEELING

The defense of FEAR

Protecting yourself through persistent feelings of eminent (emotional or physical) danger.

Most likely underlying problem: Fear of being powerless over results.
Intention of alternatives: ◊ To contain the fear; ◊ To teach you to focus on the present.

FEAR EXPRESS WAYS

- anxiety
- resistance
- reactivity
- phobias
- avoidance
- denial
- paralysis
- dread
- obsession
- control
- hesitation
- defiation
- faithlessness
- magical thinking
- negativity

ALTERNATE ROUTES

Write about fear's opposite, which is faith. How does faith work in your life? When is it most difficult to hold on to faith? What helps you reclaim faith when you have lost it?

_____
_____
_____

Be Here Now. Fear tortures you with expectations of catastrophe ("I'm not allowed to be happy and therefore something bad is inevitably going to happen to me"), magical thinking ("If I tap on the plane three times it will not crash!"), and overall a relentless terror of being out of control. Stop focusing on what might *eventually* happen and concentrate instead on this moment.

State the Obvious. Recognizing your fears and discussing those fears out loud with others, can go a long way toward debunking them and defusing their power. Talk out loud about what concerns you ("I get sick to my stomach when anyone but me is driving the car. I can't stand crowds. I constantly have horrible fantasies about my child getting hurt in some disgusting way.")

☆*Take Contrary Action*. Stop treating fear as an all-powerful deity and discover the amazing truth that (unlike actual life threatening circumstances such as walking in a dark park in most cities in the middle of the night) most fear-provoking experiences will *not* actually kill you. Instead of kowtowing to your fears, do the thing that frightens you: get on the airplane, leave your house, go to the party, change jobs, make a commitment. Write about what happens (inside) when you take these new actions.

My Personal Discoveries

My favorite alternative to Fear is: _____

An example of the way I've used this alternative is: _____

_____

The result has been: _____

_____

_____

RUN DEFENSES: DISCONNECTION THROUGH FEELING

The defense of VICTIM

Protecting yourself by focusing on feeling cheated, fooled, abused, or ignored by people and/or circumstances.

Most likely underlying problem: Fear of empowerment.
Intention of alternatives: ◊ To stop believing you are a victim; ◊ To move from being a victim to being a victor.

VICTIMIZATION EXPRESS WAYS

• fatalism	• blame	• resentment	• alarm
• confusion	• manipulation	• pessimism	• cowardice
• complaint	• withdrawal	• powerlessness	• irresponsibility
• whining	• paralysis	• chaos	• anxiety

ALTERNATE ROUTES

Write about power. Under what circumstances do you feel most powerful? What are you most afraid will happen if you come into your full power? In what specific ways would your life change?

_____

_____

_____

Thought Stop. Stop thinking "poor me" and start understanding that the world is *not* plotting against you! Write a "gratitude list" for all the wonderful things and people in your life. Read that list every day.

Get It. Always remember that you are the centerpiece of your circumstances—even when those circumstances *appear* to victimize you ("I left my job without speaking up about the way I felt," "I kept over-eating long after I became aware of the problem," "I chose an unsupportive relationship that I knew couldn't give me what I needed"). Share with another person your understanding of your contribution to your problems.

☆***Get Moving.*** The longer you wait to take action, the more difficult action becomes. Make a list of self-esteem-building activities (working out, meeting with friends, writing in a journal). Begin doing at least one such activity each day (and noting how you feel afterward).

My Personal Discoveries

My favorite alternative to Victim is: _____

An example of the way I've used this alternative is: _____

_____

The result has been: _____

_____

_____

RUN DEFENSES: DISCONNECTION THROUGH FEELING

The defense of WITHDRAWAL

Protecting yourself through emotional and even physical retreat.

Most likely underlying problem: Fear of exposure.
Intention of alternatives: ◇ To challenge the withdrawal; ◇ To encourage visibility.

WITHDRAWAL EXPRESS WAYS

• reticence	• taciturnity	• reluctance	• moodiness
• confusion	• self-abuse	• isolation	• shyness
• procrastination	• silence	• disengagement	• being tongue-tied
• retreat	• secretiveness	• rejection	• denial

ALTERNATE ROUTES

Write about what your family of origin taught you with regard to declaring your feelings? For instance, who most encouraged expression? What happened when emotions actually were shared?

_____
_____
_____

State the Obvious. Begin with a simple *statement of truth*. It doesn't need to be complicated. A plain fact is a good place to start. Say whatever comes into your mind: "I want to be alone in my room," "I don't have anything to say," "I don't know what I feel."

☆***Confront***. A lifetime of silence makes nearly every spoken truth feel confrontive—but practice quickly reduces uncomfortability. For two weeks, tell one person a day (family, friend, or stranger) what you're really *thinking*. Then for the next two weeks, tell one person a day what you're *feeling*.

Take Contrary Action. Intentional interaction is the key to change. Instead of being silent—speak up (what do you say?); when you're tempted to retreat—advance (what do you do?); rather than isolating—interact (how do you connect?).

My Personal Discoveries

My favorite alternative to Withdrawal is: _____

An example of the way I've used this alternative is: _____

_____

The result has been: _____

_____

_____

RUN DEFENSES: DISCONNECTION THROUGH FEELING

The defense of DEPRESSION

Protecting yourself through feelings of emotional, mental, and/or physical paralysis.

Most likely underlying problem: Fear of expression.
Intention of alternatives: ◇ To confront the depression; ◇ To teach you authentic expression.

DEPRESSION EXPRESS WAYS

• powerlessness	• self-abuse	• lethargy	• hopelessness
• isolation	• gloom	• sadness	• humorlessness
• withholding	• dejection	• helplessness	• eating disturbance
• withdrawing	• sorrow	• lack of sex drive	• sleep disturbance

ALTERNATE ROUTES

☆ ***Write*** about rage and/or fear (the long-avoided feelings that your lethargy and sadness are actually guarding you against). When and how do you express these two emotions? What triggers them? When and with whom does holding back seem most important?

_____

_____

_____

State the Obvious. Start with simple expressions of personal truth. Use the things that are most obvious: "I feel sad," "I feel angry," "I feel lonely," or "I feel tired."

Confront. To help avoid depression, stay current in identifying and expressing your resentments, complaints, disappointments, and angers. Tell people what you feel *as* you feel it.

Take Contrary Action. Depression is a quicksand that pulls you farther and farther down. Don't stay there and squirm! Instead of remaining in bed—go for a walk; rather than sitting around bemoaning your woes—write about what's bothering you; or instead of watching television—make a call to a friend.

My Personal Discoveries

My favorite alternative to Depression is: _____

An example of the way I've used this alternative is: _____
_____

The result has been: _____
_____
_____

RUN DEFENSES: DISCONNECTION THROUGH FEELING

The defense of TERMINAL UNIQUENESS

Protecting yourself through your feelings of being completely different from other people and through your ideas that you are therefore misperceived by them.

Most likely underlying problem: Fear of not being good enough.
Intention of alternatives: ◇ To confront the idea of terminal uniqueness; ◇ To support connectedness.

TERMINAL UNIQUENESS EXPRESS WAYS

- withholding
- judgment
- rejection
- disconnection
- fear
- isolation
- comparing
- superiority
- self-deprecation
- exclusion
- criticism
- inferiority
- alienation
- loneliness
- separateness
- complaining

ALTERNATE ROUTES

Write about the ways in which you think you're not as good as other people, and the ways in which you simply feel different from others. Write a brief history of whatever experiences have perpetuated both of these ideas. What current situations exacerbate your feelings of being different? What is your usual response to those situations?

_____
_____
_____

Tell the Truth. Find the least threatening people in your life and share with them your feelings about being left out, excluded, overlooked, unheard, and invisible.

Confront. Innuendo and partial communication reinforce disconnectedness. To defuse misconceptions speak clearly and directly about where you really stand. Ask direct questions and make precise statements with regard to your reactions and perceptions. What happens?

☆***Take Contrary Action.*** Giving up the idea that you don't belong doesn't mean giving up feeling special. Challenge such confusion if it exists. (1) When you are tempted to isolate—integrate; (2) instead of focusing on differences—note similarities; (3) rather than detaching—participate.

My Personal Discoveries

My favorite alternative to Terminal Uniqueness is: _____

An example of the way I've used this alternative is: _____
_____

The result has been: _____

RUN DEFENSES: DISCONNECTION THROUGH FEELING

The defense of SPIRITUALITY

Protecting yourself through the use of excessive religious or spiritual referencing.

Most likely underlying problem: Fear of doubt.
Intention of alternatives: ◊ To contain your spiritual sharing; ◊ To recognize your own doubt.

SPIRITUALITY EXPRESS WAYS

• arrogance	• pontification	• disconnection	• detachment
• instruction	• denial	• rejection	• dispassion
• didacticism	• self-importance	• lecturing	• condescension

ALTERNATE ROUTES

Write about your own profane, vulgar, or "improper" impulses. What is your opinion of those impulses? Where and how do you see those impulses expressed in the people around you?

_____
_____
_____

☆***Contain.*** Begin by resisting the urge to impose your spiritual constructs and concepts on others. For 60 days, *stop talking at all* about spiritual matters. Notice (and notate) what feelings arise in you during the quiet.

Disengage. Your most difficult times at first may be when you notice other people's lack of faith or sense of powerlessness. At those times you feel the need to help. The trick is to stay on your own side of the street and may resist the temptation to get involved with their problems. (This does not mean to be uncaring. It means to break the reflexive habit of *defensive* caring. When you have done that, you will see the difference and make healthy, conscious choices.)

Confront. Being truly spiritual ought not mean you are unfeeling toward others. If you find yourself ignoring, diverting, or modifying your primary emotional responses to people and/or circumstances by taking high-minded side-trips and offering unasked-for spiritual explanations, try instead sticking with your own *emotional* truth. Address and express your true body-based feeling reaction.

My Personal Discoveries

My favorite alternative to Spirituality is: _____

An example of the way I've used this alternative is: _____

The result has been: _____

RUN DEFENSES: DISCONNECTION THROUGH DOING

The defense of CHAOS

Protecting yourself through vast, disordered confusion.

Most likely underlying problem: Fear of accomplishment.
Intention of alternatives: ◇ To contain the chaos; ◇ To set the stage for accomplishment.

CHAOS EXPRESS WAYS

- compulsivity
- drama
- anxiety

- overwhelm
- confusion
- procrastination

- catastrophe
- high drama
- irritability

- excess
- disorganization
- frenetic activity

ALTERNATE ROUTES

Write about the areas in which chaos affects your life and how that chaos interferes with your accomplishments in those areas.

_____
_____
_____

Contain. This defense cannot be effectively understood or worked with until the out-of-control whirling stops. Therefore, you must do whatever is necessary to stop the pushing, confusion, and spinning—if only for a short time at first—until you can get your bearings and calm down.

Take Contrary Action. Whatever you've been doing to maintain the chaos, do the opposite (instead of staying constantly busy, spend ten minutes of the day sitting still and being quiet; rather than always saying yes to everyone and everything, tell people you'll get back to them later).

☆*Get It*. Notice the feelings that arise when there's no chaos. What feelings are they? Tell other people in your life what you're experiencing now that the chaos is gone.

My Personal Discoveries

My favorite alternative to Chaos is: _____

An example of the way I've used this alternative is: _____
_____

The result has been: _____
_____
_____

RUN DEFENSES: DISCONNECTION THROUGH DOING

The defense of COMPULSIVITY
Protecting yourself through impulsive, repetitious, self-defeating behavior.

Most likely underlying problem: Fear of your feelings of powerlessness.
Intention of alternatives: ◇ To stop the compulsive behavior; ◇ To investigate the issues underlying compulsivity.

COMPULSIVITY EXPRESS WAYS

- extravagance
- addiction
- chaos
- impulsivity
- indulgence
- repetition
- flamboyance
- delusion
- disconnection
- self-contempt
- anger
- neediness
- irrationality
- procrastination
- excess
- fear

ALTERNATE ROUTES

Write about the hole in the middle of your gut. When did you first notice it and what do you think it's about?

_____
_____
_____

☆*Contain*. Cease the compulsive action just for today. Use all the tools you can muster to do so: writing, talking to others, diversionary tactics (such as exercise), and joining with those who share your particular area of interest (like a twelve-step program).

Disengage. Compulsion is a spider web that surrounds and ensnares you. For thirty days stay clear of people and circumstances that seem to stimulate and/or reflect your particular compulsion (if you drink too much, stay away from others who drink; if you're a compulsive spender, the next time you shop, take only the cash you absolutely need and leave your checkbook and credit cards at home). Note your feelings during this time-period.

Get It. Now you can start to notice what arises when the compulsive behavior is contained. Who are you without the compulsive focus? What new feelings and thoughts have you uncovered? What do you think will happen if you continue the compulsive behavior? What do you think will happen if you stop the compulsive behavior? Record your revelations as they arise and then share your discoveries with others.

My Personal Discoveries

My favorite alternative to Compulsivity is: _____

An example of the way I've used this alternative is: _____
_____

The result has been: _____
_____
_____

RUN DEFENSES: DISCONNECTION THROUGH DOING

The defense of COUNTER-DEPENDENCE
Protecting yourself through stubborn self-reliance.

Most likely underlying problem: Fear of dependence.
Intention of alternatives: ◇ To contain the counter-dependent behavior; ◇ To provide *inter*dependent experiences.

COUNTER-DEPENDENCE EXPRESS WAYS

• isolation	• autonomy	• rejection	• over-achievement
• perfectionism	• secretive behavior	• workaholism	• overwhelm
• mistrust	• superiority	• contempt	• self-sufficiency
• rigidity	• control		

ALTERNATE ROUTES

☆ *Write* about the way your household operated when you were a child around such issues as asking for help, attitudes toward sharing, cooperation, and speaking up about needs.

_____

_____

_____

Get It. Admit to yourself the ways in which your fear of depending on others ("I don't delegate," "I don't like surprises," "I don't like gifts") affects your life. Record the general themes of your thinking with regard to these kinds of attitudes and experiences.

Confront. As a counter-dependent your experience of total control often obliterates the possibility of relationship. Expressions of authentic vulnerability, on the other hand, gives rise to the opportunity for *connection*. Learn to say exactly what you mean and to speak clearly about what you want. Tell those close to you about *your feelings* of disappointment.

Take Contrary Action. Relationship is most likely to be your key to a more fulfilling life: (1) Delegate, (2) Ask for help, (3) Invite input, (4) Allow and encourage cooperation. As always, write about your emotional responses to doing these (new) things.

My Personal Discoveries

My favorite alternative to Counter-Dependence is: _____

An example of the way I've used this alternative is: _____

_____

The result has been: _____

_____

_____

RUN DEFENSES: DISCONNECTION THROUGH DOING

The defense of PROCRASTINATION
Protecting yourself by putting things off until the last minute.

Most likely underlying problem: Fear of the responsibility that goes with accomplishment.
Intention of alternatives: ◇ To get into action; ◇ To understand the restricting fear.

PROCRASTINATION EXPRESS WAYS

- feeling overwhelm
- lethargy
- withholding
- indecisiveness
- avoidance
- rebellion
- postponing
- anxiety
- sabotage
- lack of completion
- lateness
- distractedness
- hesitation

ALTERNATE ROUTES

Write about your adolescence. What are the best and worst memories you have of that time of your life? What does being a grownup mean and how do you now feel about it?

_____

_____

_____

Confront. Discontent, hesitation, resentment, unspoken truths, and even secret dreams keep you shut down and shut off. Tell the people in your life how you feel about the way things are going—with you personally and when it comes to your relationships with them.

☆***Take Contrary Action.*** Understanding is a good beginning, but old habits die hard, so sincere effort is required if you want to change your life. Be on time. Complete projects. Speak up. Offer to help. Record your new behavior. How does it feel?

Get Moving: Make a list of what needs to be done, and do at least one thing on that list every day.

My Personal Discoveries

My favorite alternative to Procrastination is: _____

An example of the way I've used this alternative is: _____
_____

The result has been: _____
_____
_____

RUN DEFENSES: DISCONNECTION THROUGH DOING

The defense of WITHHOLDING

Protecting yourself by holding back emotionally and/or physically.

Most likely underlying problem: Fear of emotional expression.

Intention of alternatives: ◊ To release you from your withholding behavior; ◊ To provide the opportunity for emotional expression.

WITHHOLDING EXPRESS WAYS

• rejection	• sulking	• indifference	• unspoken anger
• apathy	• reticence	• sexual apathy	• extreme politeness
• withdrawal	• isolation	• repressing	• silence

ALTERNATE ROUTES

Write by making a list of your resentments. Be as thorough as possible, trying not to judge your areas of discontent as trivial, stupid, or old news. Go back as far as you can remember.

_____
_____

State the Obvious. Freedom begins with even the simplest revelation. Speak clearly and precisely in the moment. For example: "I don't know what to say," or "What I want to do is just go and hide," or "I just need to be left alone."

☆***Tell the Truth***. Silence is a hostage-taker who victimizes everyone. Even your dearest friends cannot correct what they don't realize. As soon as possible after a troubling event occurs, reveal your disappointments and annoyances to the appropriate individuals. Note the outcome as well as your response.

Take Contrary Action. Be proactive. (1) Instead of staying silent—speak up; (2) rather than rejecting ideas and experiences—take the plunge; (3) stop hiding out and choose to participate.

My Personal Discoveries

My favorite alternative to Withholding is: _____

An example of the way I've used this alternative is: _____

The result has been: _____

RUN DEFENSES: DISCONNECTION THROUGH DOING

The defense of PHYSICAL ILLNESS

Protecting yourself through constant, nagging, repetitive experiences of body problems.

Most likely underlying problem: Fear of personal power.
Intention of alternatives: ◇ To confront physical illness; ◇ To understand the relationship between your body and your mind.

PHYSICAL ILLNESS EXPRESS WAYS

- secretiveness
- control
- lethargy
- victim posture
- hypervigilance
- reluctance
- complaint
- selfishness
- whining
- isolation
- dependence
- date-breaking

ALTERNATE ROUTES

Write about how you feel in regard to personal power. If you were as powerful as you *could* be, what would your life be like? How does illness interrupt this powerful alternate possibility?

_____

_____

_____

Thought Stop. Hesitate before you allow yourself to accommodate ideas of getting sick. Substitute other types of focus. (If you're about to say "I feel a cold coming on," tell yourself to *stop* . . . then think about a project to do, call a friend and get together, or take some time off to have fun.)

☆*Get It*. Chart your personal psychological connections to illness. Keep a specific journal of what just occurred in your life (and what was on your mind) when the illness struck. (For example, a big event was approaching, a date with a new and potentially exciting individual was on the horizon, or you experienced a particular disappointment.) Write everything down—including the apparently "good" news along with what seemed negative.

Take Contrary Action. Override the overwhelm by acting "as if" (behave the way you would if things are fine). Wait twice as long as usual before giving in to your feelings of illness. (Do not, however, delay taking necessary medications. As always, seek the aid of a medical professional if a circumstance seems serious.)

My Personal Discoveries

My favorite alternative to Physical Illness is: _____

An example of the way I've used this alternative is: _____

_____

The result has been: _____
_____
_____

RUN DEFENSES: DISCONNECTION THROUGH DOING

The defense of DISSOCIATION

*Protecting yourself through an emotional separation from everything and everyone
—including separation from your own physical self.*

Most likely underlying problem: Fear of emotional over-involvement.
Intention of alternatives: ◊ To confront the dissociative behavior; ◊ To set the stage for the possibility of connection.

DISSOCIATION EXPRESS WAYS

• numbing	• withdrawing	• distractedness	• spaciness
• tuning out	• isolating	• disinterest	• apathy
• indifference	• fogginess	• boredom	• invulnerability
• separating	• disconnectedness	• disregard	• rejection

ALTERNATE ROUTES

Write about intimacy. Define it. What did intimacy look like in your home when you were growing up? When do you feel most intimate now? What is your greatest concern when it comes to intimacy?

_____
_____
_____

Be Here Now. The task is to shine a bright light into the gathering fog—immediately. Practice by thinking about that which is directly and exactly in front of you.

☆*Tell the Truth*. Fight the good fight by facing the outrageous fear. Tell the individual from whom you are most likely to hide what you are feeling and/or thinking.

Get Moving. Make a list of things you might do (or say) that feel intimate. Now, one by one, do or say those things (reveal emotion to others, share heartfelt experiences, express doubt or other threatening feelings at the moment you feel them, etc).

My Personal Discoveries

My favorite alternative to Dissociation is: _____

An example of the way I've used this alternative is: _____
_____

The result has been: _____
_____
_____

RUN DEFENSES: DISCONNECTION THROUGH THINKING

The defense of PARANOIA

Protecting yourself by assuming that people and/or circumstances are against you.

Most likely underlying problem: Fear of harm.
Intention of alternatives: ◊ To contain the paranoia; ◊ To encourage a sense of safety.

PARANOIA EXPRESS WAYS

- projecting
- self-consciousness
- hypervigilance
- victim posture

- fear
- judgment
- rejection
- anger

- secret-keeping
- negativity
- isolating
- attacking

- wariness
- loneliness
- rigidity
- criticizing

ALTERNATE ROUTES

Write about the ways in which the world feels unsafe to you. Be specific. How old were you when you first felt endangered? What was the particular nature of that danger?

_____
_____
_____

Breathe & Center. Get present. Find a pleasing image (flower, candle, joyful memory) and picture that image as being located in the center of your body. Now, breathe into that centrally located image for sixty seconds. Do this every time paranoid thoughts start to possess you.

☆***Thought Stop***. Vigilance can be an asset rather than a burden. For instance, vigilantly quiet the voices that erroneously tell you the world is against you. Say "stop" over and over again, then force your mind to travel in a new direction. ("They're *not* saying mean things about me; I'm just feeling self-conscious.")

Get It. Paranoia is a tiny cage that traps your creative energy and misdirects your attention. Consider the probability that *you*, in fact, are the actual source of your problems. Assume your paranoid thoughts are actually projections of your own self-contempt. Reverse everything: "They think I'm stupid" becomes "*I* think I'm stupid." For thirty days, keep a journal of such paranoid thoughts and their reversals.

My Personal Discoveries

My favorite alternative to Paranoia is: _____

An example of the way I've used this alternative is: _____
_____

The result has been: _____
_____
_____

RUN DEFENSES: DISCONNECTION THROUGH THINKING

The defense of GUILT
Protecting yourself by thinking you have done a bad thing.

Most likely underlying problem: Fear of being a despicable person.
Intention of alternatives: ◇ To contain the guilt; ◇ To move you toward an appreciation of yourself.

GUILT EXPRESS WAYS

- self-contempt
- regret
- negativity
- self-doubt
- constant apology
- obsession
- contrition
- penitence
- perfectionism
- over-responsibility
- remorse
- comparing
- hesitation

ALTERNATE ROUTES

Write about the way mistakes were treated in your home when you were growing up. What kinds of things were you "expected" to feel guilty about? Write about your exact thoughts with regard to your presumed essential defectiveness. How might you be considered "damaged goods" (by yourself or by others)?

_____
_____
_____

Thought Stop. Guilt boards up your windows and blocks out the sun. Instead of obsessing about your so-called failures, review your successes and contributions.

Get It. With whom (besides yourself) *might* you be angry? Be specific about the nature of the disgruntlement. Look (in writing) at the past and at the present.

☆***Tell the Truth.*** Everyone errs—but do not confuse *making* a mistake with *being* a mistake. Make a list of the things you imagine will happen if you blunder. Talk about your discoveries to other people.

My Personal Discoveries

My favorite alternative to Guilt is: _____

An example of the way I've used this alternative is: _____
_____

The result has been: _____
_____
_____

RUN DEFENSES: DISCONNECTION THROUGH THINKING

The defense of CONFUSION
Protecting yourself through emotional and/or intellectual ambivalence and disorder.

Most likely underlying problem: Fear of the consequences of being considered competent.
Intention of alternatives: ◊ To confront the confusion; ◊ To learn how to evidence your competence.

CONFUSION EXPRESS WAYS

- overwhelm
- befuddlement
- indecision
- puzzlement
- fantasy
- resignation
- lack of direction
- self-doubt
- withdrawing
- dizziness
- paralysis
- chaos

ALTERNATE ROUTES

Write about your fear of being considered competent. What do you think you would be called upon to do if you operated at full capacity? What areas of your life would change most? What losses might you incur?

_____
_____

Be Here Now. Confusion distracts you. Remember who and where you are now by breathing and focusing on the various parts and positions of your own body (my left hand is on my leg, my right foot is crossed over my left ankle).

Get It. Confusion blurs truth. Explore the payoffs of confusion (what truths might you need to face if your weren't confused). Notice (in writing) your feelings with regard to these truths.

☆*Get Moving*. Make a list of what you must do to elaborate and pursue the truths that confusion obscures (get a new job, clean my house, leave my house, etc.) Begin enacting those activities.

My Personal Discoveries

My favorite alternative to Confusion is: _____

An example of the way I've used this alternative is: _____
_____

The result has been: _____
_____
_____

RUN DEFENSES: DISCONNECTION THROUGH THINKING

The defense of INTELLECTUALIZATION

Protecting yourself through excessive analyzing, pondering, mapping, exploring, and investigating.

Most likely underlying problem: Fear of passion.
Intention of alternatives: ◇ To contain the intellectualizing; ◇ To encourage passion.

INTELLECTUALIZATION EXPRESS WAYS

- advice-giving
- over-complication
- insensitivity
- criticizing
- rigidity
- dispassion
- goal-orientation
- attacking
- controlling
- excessive planning
- arrogance
- emotionlessness

ALTERNATE ROUTES

Write about what you think would happen if passionate emotion were to influence your life strongly. How was passion regarded in your home when you were growing up. What excites you now? What ways (besides in thought) do you experience this excitement?

_____

_____

_____

☆***Contain***. You *too often* use analysis to override emotion. Refrain from criticizing, nit-picking, or advising and notice what feelings arise when you do so.

Get It. Figuring out what's wrong with everyone else is the easy part. Try instead looking at your own dismissed feelings. Then attempt to *express* those discoveries to others—even if, at first, you're only talking *about* the feelings rather than actually feeling them.

Take Contrary Action. The truly brave individual risks visibility. Instead of excusing involvement and resisting connection, do the opposite—(1) participate in events (both planned and unplanned) and find new ways to get closer to others; (2) rather than ignoring your feelings, first recognize those feelings and then express them. Notate the results.

My Personal Discoveries

My favorite alternative to Intellectualism is: _____

An example of the way I've used this alternative is: _____

_____

The result has been: _____

_____

_____

RUN DEFENSES: DISCONNECTION THROUGH THINKING

The defense of DENIAL
Protecting yourself by refusing to accept (an obvious) truth.

Most likely underlying problem: Fear of change.
Intention of alternatives: ◇ To confront your denial; ◇ To greet change.

DENIAL EXPRESS WAYS

• contradiction	• confusion	• rationalization	• irritability
• rejection	• controlling behavior	• frustration	• resentment
• rigidity	• resistance	• fantasy	• disbelief

ALTERNATE ROUTES

Write about your fear of change. What were the inconsistencies with which you were faced in childhood? How did you handle those inconsistencies?

_____
_____
_____

Thought Stop. In this case you need to stop your negative, rejecting attitude long enough to entertain the possibility that other people might be right about your excessive behavior.

☆***Get It***. Come to understand the resentments and fears that hide behind the barricade of denial. Make a list of the things that have been called to your attention. Whether or not you agree that they are a problem, keep a record of how much and how often [you drink, raise your voice, are critical, over-spend, or whatever]. If something has been pointed out to you more than twice, consider it.

Take Contrary Action. Do the opposite of whatever you've been doing (stop drinking, over-spending, raging, and rejecting).

Defense Alternatives • 133

My Personal Discoveries

My favorite alternative to Denial is: _____

An example of the way I've used this alternative is: _____
_____

The result has been: _____
_____
_____

RUN DEFENSES: DISCONNECTION THROUGH THINKING

The defense of SKEPTICISM

Protecting yourself through excessive, pervasive negativity and doubt.

Most likely underlying problem: Fear of faith and trust.
Intention of alternatives: ◊ To contain the skepticism; ◊ To practice trust.

SKEPTICISM EXPRESS WAYS

- ridicule
- contempt
- insult
- negativity
- rationalization
- disdain
- doubt
- sarcasm
- intellectualization
- didacticism
- mistrust
- vigilance
- disbelief
- rejection
- excessive analysis

ALTERNATE ROUTES

☆ *Write* about childhood disappointments. What happened to inspire your devotion to doubt?
_____
_____
_____

Contain. Stop your ridiculing and contemptuous expressions of doubt. Figure out (and notate) how you will relate to people other than through skepticism.

Tell the Truth: Discuss with someone important in your life (friend, lover, etc.) what you have discovered about the origins of your skepticism.

Get Moving. Consider ideas you have previously rejected (God exists, people care about you). Do more than think about these issues—challenge yourself with *new behavior* (go to church, share an emotional secret with a friend). Write about what happens.

My Personal Discoveries

My favorite alternative to Skepticism is: _____

An example of the way I've used this alternative is: _____

_____

The result has been: _____

_____

_____

RUN DEFENSES: DISCONNECTION THROUGH THINKING

The defense of OBSESSION

*Protecting yourself through repetitive focus on an idea, feeling, person, or thing
—a focus that most often overrides all other thinking.*

Most likely underlying problem: Fear of heartfelt connection.

Intention of alternatives: ◊ To contain the obsessive thinking; ◊ To begin experiencing reality-based connection.

OBSESSION EXPRESS WAYS

- preoccupation
- isolation
- hypervigilance
- desperation
- compulsivity
- paranoia
- rejection
- sentimentality
- chaos
- attachment
- repetition
- self-doubt

ALTERNATE ROUTES

Write about love: What is your definition of love? What were you taught about love in your family of origin? How was love communicated? How do you know when you are in love? List all of your previous important dating experiences, including length of relationships, the characteristics of your partners, and how those relationships ended. Also include a 3-4 word description of the dynamics of these relationships. Notice what patterns emerge.

_____
_____
_____

Breathe & Center. Obsession yanks you out of the-moment. Come back down to earth by first reconnecting to your own body, which will eventually make it possible for you to determine the source of your defensive behavior.

Thought Stop. Stop the mental gyrations and focus instead on what you can do to improve your life. Make a list of alternative actions you can take. Now—little by little—begin to put these behaviors into effect.

☆***Get It***. Underneath it all live a host of untold sensitivities, proclivities, susceptibilities, and (mis)perceptions. List your greatest fears: What upsets you most? Now choose someone (friend, lover, etc.) with whom to share these fears and upsets. Make a list of your best qualities? Why do you think others choose to be with you? Now actually check out your assumptions and conclusions with others.

My Personal Discoveries

My favorite alternative to Obsession is: _____

An example of the way I've used this alternative is: _____

_____

The result has been: _____

_____

_____

RUN DEFENSES: DISCONNECTION THROUGH THINKING

The defense of SELF-ABSORPTION
Protecting yourself through excessive self-centeredness.

Most likely underlying problem: Fear of being unimportant.
Intention of alternatives: ◊ To stop you from being so self-absorbed; ◊ To encourage other-directedness.

SELF-ABSORPTION EXPRESS WAYS

• exhibitionism	• indifference	• disconnectedness	• self-righteousness
• rage	• self-pity	• seductiveness	• insensitivity
• comparing	• hypervigilance	• victim posture	• hypersensitivity
• dramatizing	• complaining	• defensiveness	

ALTERNATE ROUTES

Write about where and when you first began to feel unimportant. What happened and what was your response?

_____

_____

_____

☆***Thought Stop.*** Say *stop* to self-focused thinking. Instead, direct your attention to other people, to *their* problems and circumstances.

Contain. Refrain from excess reactivity of any kind. Note (and notate) the feelings that come up when you're not raging, defending, demanding, complaining, or dramatizing circumstances.

Get Moving. Instead of complaining about your problems, make a list of ways you can be of real service to others and begin to enact items you have listed.

My Personal Discoveries

My favorite alternative to Self-Absorption is: _____

An example of the way I've used this alternative is: _____

_____

The result has been: _____

_____

_____

RUN DEFENSES: DISCONNECTION THROUGH THINKING

The defense of FANTASY

Protecting yourself through a preoccupation with illusory notions.

Most likely underlying problem: Fear of commitment.

Intention of alternatives: ◇ To contain the fantasy; ◇ To understand your relationship to commitment.

FANTASY EXPRESS WAYS

• daydreaming	• comparing	• resentment	• victim posture
• perfectionism	• disappointment	• inattentiveness	• vagueness
• lethargy	• withdrawal	• withholding	• rejection

ALTERNATE ROUTES

Write about commitment. What is it? When do you experience it? When do you hesitate? Besides fantasy, in what ways do you undermine your commitments?

_____

_____

_____

Breathe & Center. Fantasy spirits you away—out of your body and out of your life. Get back to yourself. Breathe and focus on the present moment.

☆***Thought Stop***. Your mental preoccupations are preventing you from exploring your *real* life. When you're talking with others, mentally repeat the words they're saying to you as they speak. This procedure will get you to really listen and be present to the exact situation at hand.

Confront. Fantasy begins as a reaction to discontent. Fiction seems better than fact, thereby offering the *illusion* of control. Confront this illusion by telling the people in your life how you really feel from moment to moment.

My Personal Discoveries

My favorite alternative to Fantasy is: _____

An example of the way I've used this alternative is: _____

_____

The result has been: _____

_____

_____

RUN DEFENSES: DISCONNECTION THROUGH THINKING

The defense of PERFECTIONISM
Protecting yourself by insisting upon <u>excessively</u> high standards.

Most likely underlying problem: Fear of imperfection and the abandonment you are sure will follow.
Intention of alternatives: ◇ To confront the perfectionistic attitude; ◇ To accept imperfection in yourself.

PERFECTIONISM EXPRESS WAYS

- competitiveness
- criticism
- feeling driven
- righteousness

- overwhelm
- ingratitude
- paralysis
- rigidity

- complaint
- rejection
- lack of appreciation
- self-abuse

- self-contempt
- absolutism
- vigilance
- disappointment

ALTERNATE ROUTES

Write about how your need to be perfect began (go way back!). Who in your family was perfectionistic and what did that look like to you? What is your response now when things aren't perfect? What do you think will happen if you stop trying to be perfect?

_____
_____
_____

☆ ***Contain.*** Stop exhibiting your perfectionistic bent. Repeat to yourself over and over again, "I'm not perfect; nobody else is, either; and that's okay!" Say it until you believe it—which will inevitably take longer than you think it should.

Tell the Truth. You'll need courage to let go of this defense. Investigate the fears that support your perfectionistic tendencies and then tell someone about your discoveries.

Take Contrary Action. Perfectionists live in and with complaint. Stop it. Instead try being grateful for what you're accomplishing. Also, stop when things are finished, even if they're not "perfect," invite surprise, and behave spontaneously.

My Personal Discoveries

My favorite alternative to Perfectionism is: _____

An example of the way I've used this alternative is: _____
_____

The result has been: _____
_____
_____

CHAPTER 4

THE DEFENSE RESOURCES

Understand that all events—whether internal or external—are ultimately subjective. That is, they are *processed* internally and are seen through a personal *emotional and mental* lens. Think of yourself as wearing special glasses—glasses that show you the world in a particular light and color. Everything you see and know is filtered through whatever unique kind of vision those glasses allow. You don't, for instance, necessarily agree with everyone else on what or who is really beautiful because, as the well-known saying declares, "beauty is in the eye of the beholder." And similarly, everyone doesn't agree with you about which music is good or what actor is the best, because your viewpoint is . . . your *view point*. Thus, though you may sometimes be swept up in the general, collective view of something or another—or may agree on the general facts of a circumstance—your opinions and reactions still vary from those of other people *because of the lens through which you perceive the situation*. What you must do, therefore, is look beyond the apparent facts and discover the *impact* of those apparent facts on your individual circumstances.

Workout #3

What you *perceive* a situation to be is as important as the so-called facts. Change your viewpoint and everything will feel different.

This is not to say there are no facts. This is only to say that *much more important than the facts will always be your interpretation of those facts,* as well as your immediate and then ongoing application of that interpretation (*Fact*: "Mother spanked me and left me alone." *Interpretation*: "Mother didn't love me." *Immediate reaction*: "I closed up." *Ongoing application*: "Whenever someone seems miffed at me or discontented, I close up.")

Therefore, if you concentrate only on getting the facts in order, you will still be left feeling that you have resolved little. This is why you can stop going on any more fact-finding missions and focus instead on your interpretation of the facts as you understand them to have existed, and on your ongoing application of that interpretation. You will get the most from recognizing how your *reactions* affect your life (and how those reactions affect the people in your life).

A picture of your defensive patterns has really taken shape by now. You have come to understand which defenses you've been using and how you've been using them, as well as what new actions you can take to gain authority over the troublesome or limiting aspects of those defenses.

Of course, seeing these defenses as problems—as behaviors, thoughts, or feeling responses that have impeded or tangled up your life—is easy. Equally important, however, is recognizing and understanding that, along the way, as you established these defenses, you simultaneously developed some corresponding worthy and useful habits of thinking, feeling, and behavior. In fact, *each* defense encourages certain (now well-developed) habit patterns that can offer you a surprising amount of support and assistance, if you elect to use them consciously and in support of your well-being.

Realize, then, how the characteristics you developed in the course of building your defense patterns can and do *enhance* your life.

To appreciate this enhancement, you can use the material in this chapter to examine:

The Resources: Substantial "positive" consequences of particular defensive habits. At least two are noted for each defense. Many more exist, and I recommend that you add your own as you become aware of them.

The Important Modifiers: Balancing characteristics or attitudes that help either soften or expand the impact of that Resource.

(Please note that I have made no attempt to discuss either the Resources or the Modifiers in any detail. Rather, what I offer is a reference point that encourages appreciation for *all* defensive developments.)

> *Note: For each defense, space has been provided where you can, if you wish, write in your own Resources and Modifiers.*

HIT DEFENSES: CONNECTION THROUGH FEELING

The defense of ANGER

RESOURCE	MODIFIER
PASSION. Intensity, vehemence, and fervor can all be displays of anger. They are also indicators of passion! Passion is a foundation for everything, from amazing relationships to astonishing art.	**RESTRAINT.** Expressing your passion is essential, but *unrestrained* passion often results in a chaos that sabotages success by distracting you from your goals.
OUTSPOKENNESS. Defensive anger, though often more outrageous than communicative, has taught you how to speak up.	**DISCRETION.** You need to learn *when* speaking up is appropriate and also how to address the *underlying* feelings that have inspired your anger.

The defense of CONTEMPT FOR OTHERS

RESOURCE	MODIFIER
DISCERNMENT. Contempt has developed in you an exquisite ability for emotional discrimination. Now you can (non-defensively) evaluate the people who come into your life today.	**ACCEPTANCE.** Overlooking the flaws and frailties in those around you is essential; otherwise, you'll constantly find that *no one* is good enough in your eyes.
IRREVERENCE. Through your contrariness, you have evolved strong personal opinions and resolves.	**REVERENCE.** Learn to respect *other* people's opinions in order to increase your own understanding. More heads are very often better than one!

If either defense above is familiar to you, write your own favorite Resource and/or Modifier here:

_____   _____

_____   _____

_____   _____

HIT DEFENSES: CONNECTION THROUGH FEELING & DOING

The defense of BLAME

RESOURCE	MODIFIER
PERCEPTIVITY. In order to blame, you've needed to investigate the habits and characteristics of the people in your life and to recognize their shortcomings. This has taught you to identify others' various qualities quickly.	**SELF-EXAMINATION.** Now, look in the mirror and use your skills to investigate your own complicity in the difficulties of your life.
EGO MODIFICATION. You probably have an inherent tendency to aggrandize and glorify other people. Blame has helped you keep a handle on this tendency.	**APPRECIATION.** Don't forget to acknowledge in yourself the qualities you applaud (or loathe!) in others.

The defense of SPILLING

RESOURCE	MODIFIER
ARTICULATION. All of that overflowing chatter probably contained kernels of wisdom. Now you can share that wisdom in more hearable ways.	**BOUNDARIES.** While sharing thoughts and feelings, it is essential that you develop a consciousness with regard to the impact of your words.
SOCIABILITY. You're most likely known as a "people person"—someone who interacts comfortably with others.	**INTIMACY.** Speaking from the heart can allow simple interactions to become great relationships.

If either defense above is familiar to you, write your own favorite Resource and/or Modifier here:

_____   _____

_____   _____

_____   _____

HIT DEFENSES: CONNECTION THROUGH DOING

The defense of GOSSIP

RESOURCE	MODIFIER
RECEPTIVITY. As a gossip, you learned to recognize strengths and weaknesses in others.	**CONSTRAINT.** Learn to share some *but not all* of your observations. Do this and you will turn a negative habit into a positive proactive trait.
STORY-TELLING ABILITY. You have become an excellent storyteller. Eliminate the vitriol, envy, and deceit, and what's left will be great communication.	**SENSITIVITY.** To be most successful as a storyteller, keep your eye on your listeners, recognizing their individual peculiarities, predispositions, and hesitations.

The defense of HUMOR

RESOURCE	MODIFIER
INTUITION. Humor at its best requires that you develop uncommon insight and a special ability to notice what others often miss about a situation.	**RESTRAINT.** Sometimes your great insights should be shared . . . but many times holding your tongue is a better idea.
LAUGHTER. Nothing heals like laughter, especially when it is free of cruel or denigrating anger.	**CONSCIOUSNESS.** Be certain to stay awake to the impact of what you're saying and guard against humor that might feel ridiculing or insulting to others.

If either defense above is familiar to you, write your own favorite Resource and/or Modifier here:

_____   _____

_____   _____

_____   _____

HIT DEFENSES: CONNECTION THROUGH DOING

The defense of DEPENDENCE

RESOURCE	MODIFIER
TRUST. As a dependent person, you have learned to rely on others—a rare and important skill!	**SELF-ESTEEM.** What begins as an ability to rely on others can quickly turn into an unhealthy, draining neediness when you have little or no faith in yourself.
LEARNING ABILITY. Depending on others has taught you how to take in new important information.	**ASSESSMENT.** Having the ability to take in new information does not mean swallowing *everything* you're told. Think for yourself. Determine what's valuable for you as well as what's not.

The defense of CODEPENDENCE

RESOURCE	MODIFIER
CARING. Codependence has taught you how to be considerate, thoughtful, and nurturing. These qualities go far in establishing fulfilling relationships.	**RECEIVING.** Learning how to accept and appreciate the gifts others can give to you will further enhance your giving ability.
GENEROSITY. Your focus on making everyone else happy has taught you generosity. Absent the need to control people and events, this generosity can be a great attribute.	**BOUNDARIES.** Acknowledge *your own* needs! Say "No!" more often, and think before saying anything at all.

If either defense above is familiar to you, write your own favorite Resource and/or Modifier here:

_____   _____

_____   _____

_____   _____

HIT DEFENSES: CONNECTION THROUGH DOING

The defense of THERAPIZING

RESOURCE	MODIFIER
NURTURING ABILITY. Through therapizing, you've learned how to nourish, support, discern, and comprehend.	**CONTAINMENT.** But there's a narrow line between enthusiastic encouragement and overwhelming expectation, between helpfulness and enabling, between protection and obstruction.
PROBLEM ANALYZING. All that advice-giving is evidence of your real ability to figure out and understand problems.	**AWARENESS.** Giving advice is fine. Unasked-for advice, however, is very often inappropriate. Make certain you're invited to intercede.

The defense of CONTROL

RESOURCE	MODIFIER
CONFIDENCE. Your ability to be assertive has developed in you a healthy sense of rightful personal authority.	**MODESTY.** Recognize your limitations. You don't need to express your opinion in every situation.
MANAGEMENT SKILLS. You have a great capacity to run the show.	**COMPROMISE.** Soften your tendency to be absolute, and that ability will blossom.

If either defense above is familiar to you, write your own favorite Resource and/or Modifier here:

_____   _____

_____   _____

_____   _____

HIT DEFENSES: CONNECTION THROUGH DOING & THINKING

The defense of CRITICISM

RESOURCE	MODIFIER
EVALUATIVE ABILITY. You have developed the capacity to assess the qualities of both circumstances and people. Now do this confidently and quickly.	**ENCOURAGEMENT.** It's easy to focus on the holes and forget to admire the overall quality, flavor, and shape of the cheese. Since assessment without appreciation can be soulless, add some kind thoughts to your evaluations.
VIGILANCE. In order to notice what's wrong, you've needed to maintain a watchful eye. Now you're extraordinary alert.	**EASE.** Sometimes it's important to relax your vigilance long enough to savor the unexpected, and to enjoy surprises.

The defense of PROJECTION

RESOURCE	MODIFIER
This most common of all defenses has but one obvious resource, but that resource is so important and powerful that a thorough appreciation and use of it is absolutely life-changing.	
INSIGHT INTO OTHERS. All this time spent noticing (and rejecting) other people has helped you learn to understand how they really work.	**INTROSPECTION.** Your observations about other people ("He's selfish. She's a wimp. He's powerful. She's extraordinary.") are actually often recognitions of feelings or behaviors *you* have but often neglect to recognize, appreciate or accept. Take a good look at yourself.

If either defense above is familiar to you, write your own favorite Resource and/or Modifier here:

_____   _____

_____   _____

_____   _____

HIT DEFENSES: CONNECTION THROUGH DOING

The defense of JUDGMENT

RESOURCE	MODIFIER
PRINCIPLES. You have developed a value system—a consistent set of standards from which to operate. This value system offers you freedom from a chaotic, haphazard life.	**FLEXIBILITY.** Now try entertaining alternative (even novel) concepts. Remember that other people also have useful information to offer you.
DISCERNMENT. Successful individuals are able to detect inconsistencies and then adjust. Judgment has taught you to do this as well.	**ACCEPTANCE.** Temper judgment with understanding compassion. We're all flawed.

The defense of COMPARING

RESOURCE	MODIFIER
EVALUATIVE ABILITY. You have become accomplished at recognizing what's what.	**INTROSPECTION.** Now focus on your own conduct rather than the conduct of others.
APPRECIATION. Long-practiced habits of careful observation have taught you to admire the qualities, capacities, and results achieved by others.	**SELF-ESTEEM.** Don't forget to appreciate what's great about you!

If either defense above is familiar to you, write your own favorite Resource and/or Modifier here:

_____   _____

_____   _____

_____   _____

HIT DEFENSES: CONNECTION THROUGH DOING

The defense of ANALYZING

RESOURCE	MODIFIER
DETERMINATION. Analyzing teaches you surefootedness as you move from one point to another, then finally to a decision. Decision-making ability is essential in order to have a functional life.	**FEELINGS.** Every truly clever conclusion must be tempered with compassion. Don't overlook the value of the very real information conveyed in feelings. Learn to check in on your own emotional state.
DEPTH. Through constant analyzing, you have developed a skill for delving beneath the surface of things.	**CONTAINMENT.** Be certain you're invited to present your discoveries.

The defense of MASKING

RESOURCE	MODIFIER
SOCIALIZATION. You've learned how to adapt to a variety of circumstances and can usually, therefore, easily fit in anywhere.	**SELF-AWARENESS.** It helps, however, to don your mask with will and consciousness—that is, to do so because you *want* to, not because you have to.
SELF-PROTECTION. The ability to hide from prying eyes and prevent unwanted discovery. Screening out undesirable intrusion can be a welcome protection in an all-too-often intrusive world.	**DECLARATION.** But Masking is most helpful when it's a *choice* rather than a mandate.

If either defense above is familiar to you, write your own favorite Resource and/or Modifier here:

_____   _____

_____   _____

_____   _____

RUN DEFENSES: DISCONNECTION THROUGH FEELING

The defense of SHAME

RESOURCE	MODIFIER
MODESTY. Shame prevents your ego from becoming inflated and destructive. Healthy shame (appropriately) modifies behavior.	**HEALTHY SELF-ESTEEM.** Excessive modesty can easily turn into gross, negative, paralyzing self-consciousness.
BOUNDARIES. Shame tends to contain your behavior the way a fence encloses a yard.	**SPONTANEITY.** Within your shame-inspired limits and boundaries, remember to occasionally let the dog run wild in that fenced yard of yours.

The defense of SELF-CONTEMPT

RESOURCE	MODIFIER
HUMILITY. Self-contempt has reigned in any potential arrogance you might have and helped you to resist the temptation to be "full of yourself."	**HEALTHY PRIDE.** Self-contempt without modification is certain to undermine your potential success in almost every area of life.
RESPONSIBILITY. Self-contempt alerts you to your own accountability.	**SPONTANEITY.** Still, at times you must act unselfconsciously in order to experience full joy.

If either defense above is familiar to you, write your own favorite Resource and/or Modifier here:

_____   _____

_____   _____

_____   _____

RUN DEFENSES: DISCONNECTION THROUGH FEELING

The defense of FEAR

RESOURCE	MODIFIER
BEHAVIORAL CONTAINMENT. Even while it holds you back, fear teaches you the necessity of imposing important boundaries on your life.	**FAITH.** The great modifier for your fear is faith—belief that you're protected in ways that are not immediately obvious to you. Often fear is more about your need to control outcomes than about real danger.
REVERENCE. Dread is the great monitor of behavior, insisting that you conduct yourself with a certain cautious reverence. Fear, then, sets off the alarms that can guide you and even guard you from potential harm.	**BOLDNESS.** But too much reserve stomps out your natural fire, thereby limiting your horizons and also your potential contributions. Finally, you need to go where angels fear to tread.

The defense of VICTIM

RESOURCE	MODIFIER
PATIENCE. As a victim, you got used to waiting for something helpful to happen. Now you know how to bide your time.	**CONSCIOUS INTENTION.** Recognize the difference between a patiently accepting circumstances and simply withholding effort.
ENDURANCE. Usually it is real events that have helped you feel like a victim, and through those events you've learned how to withstand hardship.	**PROACTIVITY.** Now is the time to apply your ability to persevere. Take action and face the sometimes alarming experiences or feelings that accompany new behavior.

If either defense above is familiar to you, write your own favorite Resource and/or Modifier here:

_____   _____

_____   _____

_____   _____

RUN DEFENSES: DISCONNECTION THROUGH FEELING

The defense of WITHDRAWAL

RESOURCE	MODIFIER
RESTRAINT. Years of curbing, bridling, and restricting yourself have taught you to modify not only what you say, but also how and when you speak.	**IMPULSIVITY.** To release yourself from the inner ties that bind, you must learn to sometimes act without first weighing all the odds.
DETACHMENT. You have an ability to remain free of emotional attachment (especially to outcomes). This wise, unbiased, observer's stance makes you a helpful listener.	**INVOLVEMENT.** However, without a sense of connectedness, you can easily fall into the trap of feeling distant, even arrogant, superiority.

The defense of DEPRESSION

RESOURCE	MODIFIER
HUMILITY. Often depression can feel defeating—an experience that, appropriately applied, can teach humility.	**SELF-SATISFACTION.** Still, too much humility is no good, either. Remember to appreciate the things about yourself that legitimately deserve appreciation (your kindness, thoughtfulness, promptness, follow-through, and humor).
FOCUS. When you're depressed, each moment seems endless. This apparent slowing of time can teach you to stay in the moment.	**OVERVIEW.** If you focus too much on the moment and forget to also look ahead, you may come to a dead halt. While attending to the present, keep your eye on the future.

If either defense above is familiar to you, write your own favorite Resource and/or Modifier here:

_____   _____

_____   _____

_____   _____

RUN DEFENSES: DISCONNECTION THROUGH FEELING

The defense of TERMINAL UNIQUENESS

RESOURCE	MODIFIER
OBSERVATIONAL POWER. You've become a wonderful detective who notices distinguishing qualities and attitudes.	**VERIFICATION.** Unfortunately your assumptions about how others feel and what they perceive are often erroneous. Check them out!
DISCERNMENT. You've learned to recognize what's special about yourself and about others.	**CONNECTION.** Sometimes, however, you turn distinction into disconnection. Put yourself in the shoes of others and focus more on what connects you *to* them than on what separates you *from* them.

The defense of SPIRITUALITY

RESOURCE	MODIFIER
FAITH. Spiritual practice teaches the value of belief.	**SKEPTICISM.** But it's easy to be blind to aspects of reality that need to be seen. Stay alert to ego influences (other people's and your own).
TRUST. You've learned to believe that things turn out the way they should.	**FOOTWORK.** Even as you have genuine faith that life will work out well, remember that if you don't take action, things won't get done.

If either defense above is familiar to you, write your own favorite Resource and/or Modifier here:

_____   _____
_____   _____
_____   _____

RUN DEFENSES: DISCONNECTION THROUGH DOING

The defense of CHAOS

RESOURCE	MODIFIER
FLEXIBILITY. Chaos has taught you how to adjust to different, often rapidly changing situations.	**ROUTINE.** Stop spinning. Focus instead on one thing at a time. Routine helps calm life's whirlwinds.
SPONTANEITY. Chaos often necessitates your coming up with an immediate, intuitive response. Thus, you've learned how to respond unhesitatingly.	**INTENTION.** Spontaneity puts spark in (over-organized) routine, but well-devised intention adds purposeful drive to your life.

The defense of COMPULSIVITY

RESOURCE	MODIFIER
ABUNDANCE. As a compulsive, you tend to assume there's plenty more where that came from!	**SATISFACTION.** Allow yourself satisfaction with what you already have. Free yourself from the nauseous yearning that has so often left you needing more.
FOCUS. When you wanted to satisfy your fleeting desires, there was no stopping you. Now, from that practice, you know how to meet significant goals successfully.	**OVERVIEW.** But if the intensity of your focus obscures the bigger picture, it limits your ability to succeed. Carefully distinguish what seems important from what really is important.

If either defense above is familiar to you, write your own favorite Resource and/or Modifier here:

_____   _____

_____   _____

_____   _____

Defense Resources • 157

RUN DEFENSES: DISCONNECTION THROUGH DOING

The defense of COUNTER-DEPENDENCE

RESOURCE	MODIFIER
RESOLVE. As a counter-dependent, you have honed the ability to be decisive, determined, and persistent.	**FLEXIBILITY.** Your great resolve gives you a feeling of considerable control, but also brings you great burden. Free yourself by allowing others to influence and contribute to your decisions.
RESPONSIBILITY. Above all else, the counter-dependent knows how to take care of business and honor obligations.	**PLAYFULNESS.** But all work and no play most often undermines productivity. Balance is the key.

The defense of PROCRASTINATION

RESOURCE	MODIFIER
PACING. As a procrastinator, you took an easygoing approach to your life, which can result in a relaxed sense of timing.	**RESOLVE.** In order to create an effective plan, good timing needs to be combined with fearless intention.
PATIENCE. The procrastinator—accustomed to waiting until the last minute—learns to wait things out.	**ACTIVITY.** Don't confuse a sensible take-it-easy attitude with resignation or total sloth, otherwise your so-called patience can quickly turn to total shutdown. Focus on getting things done.

If either defense above is familiar to you, write your own favorite Resource and/or Modifier here:

_____   _____

_____   _____

RUN DEFENSES: DISCONNECTION THROUGH DOING

The defense of WITHHOLDING

RESOURCE	MODIFIER
RESTRAINT. As a withholder you've learned the value of waiting until you can present yourself to others in the most appropriate and acceptable ways.	**AUDACITY.** There are times when speaking boldly without worrying about what's most appropriate can inspire those around you while at the same time empowering you. Be brave and speak up.
NON-REACTIVITY. Silence has taught you how to take the time you need to respond rather than react.	**THOROUGH RESPONSIVENESS.** Your ability to draw the line can too easily turn into a habit of non-communication. Keep your eyes open and watch for your old tendency to respond *automatically* . . . with silence.

The defense of PHYSICAL ILLNESS

RESOURCE	MODIFIER
PACING. Illness slows you down and teaches you how to rest.	**RESOLVE.** Figure out if you're really pacing yourself, or if, instead, you're merely giving up.
FLEXIBILITY. Illness has taught you how to adjust to circumstances.	**PURPOSEFULNESS.** It can become all too easy to lose track of your goal. Stay flexible but determined.

If either defense above is familiar to you, write your own favorite Resource and/or Modifier here:

_____   _____

_____   _____

_____   _____

RUN DEFENSES: DISCONNECTION THROUGH DOING & THINKING

The defense of DISSOCIATION

RESOURCE	MODIFIER
IMPARTIALITY. Habitual defensive uninvolvement teaches you to override your own biases.	**PASSION.** Ardor and intensity lend color to the blank face of the impartial individual, and transforms detachment to involved awareness.
WITNESS ABILITY. Dissociation can initiate a state of calm—teaching you to keep your head when chaos is erupting all around you.	**INVOLVEMENT.** Still you're likely to be tempted to stay so separate that important emotional connection gets overlooked.

The defense of PARANOIA

RESOURCE	MODIFIER
ALERTNESS. Constantly watching for pitfalls, predators and problems activates a warning device inside you that protects you from stumbling obliviously into trouble.	**IMPULSIVITY.** Allowing yourself to respond in unpremeditated ways will introduce a sense of freedom (and probably creativity) into your life.
KEEN OBSERVATION. Vigilance develops your ability to recognize things that others often miss.	**OVERVIEW.** Keep your eye on the big picture (context) as well as on the details of the story (content), for the net of minutia can easily entangle you and drag you down.

If either defense above is familiar to you, write your own favorite Resource and/or Modifier here:

_____   _____

_____   _____

_____   _____

RUN DEFENSES: DISCONNECTION THROUGH THINKING

The defense of GUILT

RESOURCE	MODIFIER
RESPONSIBILITY. Guilt refines your ability to assess your personal accountability.	**SELF-APPRECIATION.** As important as recognizing your mistakes is appreciating your assets and contributions.
BOUNDARIES. Guilt prevents naked table-dancing, stealing, and other expressions of (often destructive) excess and unethical conduct.	**RISK.** Monitoring your own behavior can be immobilizing. In order to grow, you must be willing to take risks.

The defense of CONFUSION

RESOURCE	MODIFIER
LEARNING ABILITY. In the middle of your confusion you most likely ask many questions. This is fundamental to learning.	**GROUNDING.** If you can learn to keep your feet on the ground and avoid getting caught in the (apparent) whirlwinds of your life, you're likely to accomplish your goals.
ADAPTABILITY. Confusion has trained you to stay upright in the midst of muddle.	**DECISIVENESS.** Trusting *your own* sense of direction and intention keeps you from becoming excessively accommodating.

If either defense above is familiar to you, write your own favorite Resource and/or Modifier here:

_____   _____

_____   _____

_____   _____

RUN DEFENSES: DISCONNECTION THROUGH THINKING

The defense of INTELLECTUALIZATION

RESOURCE	MODIFIER
COMPREHENSION SKILLS. Figuring everything out all the time has taught you to do just that!	**SENSATIONS.** Do not, however, underestimate the importance of emotional values and influences. Pure intellect—insofar as it excludes sensations, feelings, instinct and intuition—robs experience of dimension.
ACCESS TO TRUTH. The intellectual tends to approach circumstances with a certain candor.	**EMPATHY.** Learn to put yourself in the other persons place and to feel their difficulty. Facts are only part of the truth picture. The *truth* also includes our feelings about those facts.

The defense of DENIAL

RESOURCE	MODIFIER
TENACITY. You need a strong will to stick to notions rejected by others. You have such a will.	**FLEXIBILITY.** Learn to entertain new and conflicting ideas.
CONFRONTATION. You've learned to speak up in defense of positions you favor or support.	**ACKNOWLEDGMENT.** From time to time, you must admit the possibility that opposing viewpoints may exist, and may even have some truth to them!

If either defense above is familiar to you, write your own favorite Resource and/or Modifier here:

_____   _____

_____   _____

_____   _____

RUN DEFENSES: DISCONNECTION THROUGH THINKING

The defense of SKEPTICISM

RESOURCE	MODIFIER
PREPAREDNESS. You're alert to danger—both intellectual and actual.	**FAITH.** However, your skepticism often brings with it negativity and hopelessness. Faith (in something greater than yourself) offers positivity and hope.
RATIONALITY. Your rational inquiry provides you with important logical information.	**INNER GUIDANCE.** Dropping your intellectual guard will bring flavor to a bland life. Let intuition and instinct influence your perspective.

The defense of OBSESSION

RESOURCE	MODIFIER
PERSEVERANCE. You've insistently determined you have a great ability to concentrate on achieving what you regard as important.	**MODERATION.** Ignoring everything (but your focus) limits accomplishment. Seek balance.
IMAGINATION. The fantasy of obsession has expanded your contemplative ability, as well as your creative capacity.	**REALITY.** Learn to recognize the difference between fantasy and reality. What's real (and fine) in your life.

If either defense above is familiar to you, write your own favorite Resource and/or Modifier here:

_____   _____

_____   _____

_____   _____

RUN DEFENSES: DISCONNECTION THROUGH THINKING

The defense of SELF-ABSORPTION

RESOURCE	MODIFIER
SELF-ANALYSIS. While thinking so much about yourself you've learned how to . . . think about yourself! This can lead to self-understanding.	**EMPATHY.** Now take your focus off *your* own concerns, and instead consider *other people's* concerns. Try imagining what they are feeling or needing.
INITIATING. Your need to be the center of focus has taught you how to motivate people to pay attention.	**SHARING.** It's also important to be able to sit back and let others have the limelight.

The defense of FANTASY

RESOURCE	MODIFIER
VISION. Living in a world of fantasy has expanded and nurtured your ability to be creative.	**GROUNDEDNESS.** Too much fantasy impedes normal progress and real accomplishment. Try to stay in the present, keeping today's intentions clear.
OVERVIEW. Fantasy has taught you how to escape getting bogged down in the details of the moment.	**REALITY.** But those same details are often actually the "trials of daily life," and thus cannot and should not be avoided or ignored. Acknowledge the importance of those "trials" by giving them the attention they deserve.

If either defense above is familiar to you, write your own favorite Resource and/or Modifier here:

_____   _____

_____   _____

_____   _____

RUN DEFENSES: DISCONNECTION THROUGH THINKING

The defense of PERFECTIONISM

RESOURCE	MODIFIER
MOTIVATION. For a long time you've been driven to achieve things. This drive will be a valuable asset to you as you move through the world and seek further success.	**ACCEPTANCE.** Accepting your own (inevitable) mistakes will help you accept the mistakes of others.
ASSESSMENT. Your years of criticizing and of being vigilant have taught you to notice what works best (and what doesn't work at all).	**SATISFACTION.** Now, stop focusing on what's missing. Appreciate what you have and what you do.

If either defense above is familiar to you, write your own favorite Resource and/or Modifier here:

_____   _____

_____   _____

_____   _____

AT LAST

This has been quite a journey we've taken together. By now, you have hopefully put into action some of the recommended Defense Busters. Perhaps, then, you have come to see that your life can feel *and be* different. You can make that difference a reality!

After all is said and done, however, there is a final step in the process of change. It involves learning how to *appreciate the life you are living now*—how to find a satisfaction with that life. This satisfaction, when experienced honestly and thoroughly, allows you to approach your days with contentment—while still aiming toward more and more actualization of your potential.

Workout #4

First be happy with who you are, where you are, and what you have—and *then* aim for more. Fight the good fight.

I leave you with a final story—a tender, simple story about a busboy who, in a profound way, understands better than most this final step in the process of change.

THE BUSBOY

Many years ago several friends and I were having dinner in a well-known Los Angeles artists' hangout—a restaurant—where most of the servers and bartenders are hopefuls struggling to earn a living while pursuing fame and fortune. On this particular night, my friends and I were greeted by a "waiter" obviously none too happy with his situation, which he clearly regarded as demeaning. In contrast with his unpleasantness was the extraordinary and gentle sincerity coming from the young busboy, who patiently assisted the waiter, while also ignoring the waiter's constant complaints.

This busboy was so solicitous, genuine, and endearing that I was finally moved to say to him, "That waiter is so mean. How in the world can you stand working with him?"

"Oh, he's not a waiter," the busboy replied.

"He's not," I wondered. "What is he?"

"He's a songwriter," the boy said with enthusiasm and admiration.

"A songwriter!" I quoted, "I see. And what are you?"

"Me?" he returned, his eyes glistening proudly. "I'm a busboy." He paused, then added, "but I *want* to be a waiter." Whereupon he handed me a business card with his name on it . . . and the title "Busboy."

I wish you satisfaction in your life and joy in your journey.

APPENDIX A
FIFTEEN STEPS IN DEFENSE BUSTING

Step 1

Identify the childhood patterns that still color your life.

Step 2

Recognize and appreciate your own particular, natural style.

Step 3

Understand that what you have is what you (unconsciously) want.

Step 4

Realize that *all* behavior has a payoff.

Step 5

Realize that feeling safe is an inside job.

Step 6

Notice the way yesterday's ideas are affecting today's happiness.

Step 7

Realize that the *defense itself* is not the actual problem. The actual problem is that you have made an *inner connection* between the defense and the pain-filled fears that originally called the defense into play.

Step 8

Uncover the basic *stories* in which you are stuck. To do this, look at your relationship with your father, with your mother, and with yourself as a child.

Step 9

Realize: the bigger your reaction, the older the memory inspiring that reaction.

Step 10

Dig deep. Figure out which defenses you use most, recognize the origin of the defenses, and notice how they are now appearing in your life.

Step 11

Are you chained to old ideas? Wrapped up in false self-concepts? Discover the specific ways you keep yourself attached to the past.

Step 12

Take the work of growth and discovery seriously, and take yourself lightly!

Step 13

Realize that all conscious feeling and thinking themes are inevitably balanced by equal and opposite *unconscious* feeling and thinking themes. Look for the opposites in yourself

Step 14

Notice how expectation leads to manifestation. In other words, what you expect, you get. So if you're watching every step you take because you expect to fall—you can expect to fall!

Step 15

Realize that change is a matter of choice.

APPENDIX B
CORRELATIONS BY DEFENSE

Each of the forty-one major defenses is listed below (in alphabetical order) along with three of the 14 Solutions that are likely to be most effective in dealing with it. Not included among these Solutions are three that will <u>always</u> be useful for <u>every</u> defense: #2 (Rouse), #3 (Meditate), and #4 (Write).

Analyzing	#6: Direct Statements	#10: Show Up	#14: Take Contrary Action
Anger	#4: Breathe & Center	#6: Direct Statements	#9: Disengage
Blame	#5: Tell the Truth	#11: Thought Stop	#12: Contain
Chaos	#10: Show Up	#12: Contain	#:13: Ground
Codependence	#8: Confront	#9: Disengage	#14: Take Contrary Action
Comparing	#6: Direct Statements	#11: Thought Stop	#15: Get into Action
Compulsivity	#4: Breathe & Center	#10: Show Up	#12: Contain
Confusion	#8: Confront	#13: Ground	#15: Get into Action
Contempt	#11: Thought Stop	#12: Contain	#14: Take Contrary Action
Controlling	#5: Tell the Truth	#10: Show Up	#14: Take Contrary Action
Counter-dependence	#6: Direct Statements	#8: Confront	#10: Show Up
Criticism	#5: Tell the Truth	#12: Contain	#14: Take Contrary Action
Denial	#6: Direct Statements	#10: Show Up	#14: Take Contrary Action
Dependence	#6: Direct Statements	#14: Take Contrary Action	#15: Get into Action
Depression	#7: State the Obvious	#8: Confront	#14: Take Contrary Action
Dissociation	#5: Tell the Truth	#13: Ground	#15: Get into Action
Fantasy	#4: Breathe & Center	#10: Show Up	#11: Thought Stop
Fear	#4: Breathe & Center	#11: Thought Stop	#14: Take Contrary Action
Gossip	#6: Direct Statements	#12: Contain	#14: Take Contrary Action
Guilt	#5: Tell the Truth	#10: Show Up	#11: Thought Stop
Humor	#11: Thought Stop	#12: Contain	#14: Take Contrary Action

Intellectualization	#5: Tell the Truth	#11: Thought Stop	#12: Contain
Judging	#10: Show Up	#11: Thought Stop	#15: Get into Action
Masking	#5: Tell the Truth	#6: Direct Statements	#8: Confront
Obsession	#4: Breathe & Center	#5: Tell the Truth	#11: Thought Stop
Paranoia	#4: Breathe & Center	#10: Show Up	#11: Thought Stop
Perfectionism	#9: Disengage	#10: Show Up	#12: Contain
Physical Illness	#8: Confront	#10: Show Up	#11: Thought Stop
Procrastination	#8: Confront	#14: Take Contrary Action	#15: Get into Action
Projecting	#8: Confront	#10: Show Up	#14: Take Contrary Action
Self-contempt	#8: Confront	#10: Show Up	#14: Take Contrary Action
Shame	#10: Show Up	#12: Contain	#14: Get into Action
Skepticism	#:5: Tell the Truth	%10: Show Up	#12: Contain
Spilling	#4: Breathe & Center	#5: Tell the Truth	#12: Contain
Spirituality	#5: Tell Truth	#6: Direct Statements	#12: Contain
Terminal Uniqueness	#5: Tell the Truth	#6: Direct Statements	#14: Take Contrary Action
Therapizing	#9: Disengage	#12: Contain	#14: Take Contrary Action
Victimization	#10: Show Up	#11: Thought Stop	#15: Get into Action
Withdrawn	#7: State the Obvious	#8: Confront	#14: Take Contrary Action
Withholding	#5: Tell the Truth	#7: State the Obvious	#15: Get into Action

APPENDIX C
CORRELATIONS BY SYMPTOM

Each of the following familiar, defense-related symptoms (listed in alphabetical order) is shown alongside two of the 14 Solutions that are likely to be most effective in dealing with it. Not included among these Solutions are three that will <u>always</u> be useful for <u>every</u> symptom: #2 (Rouse), #3 (Meditate), and #4 (Write).

Anxiety	#1: Breathe & Center	#11: Thought Stop
Babbling	#12: Contain	#13: Ground
Boundarilessness	#9: Disengage	#8: Confront
Clumsiness	#13: Ground	#4: Breathe & Center
Condescension	#6: Direct Statements	#10: Show Up
Convincing	#9: Disengage	#12: Contain
Covert behavior	#6: Direct Statements	#5: Tell the Truth
Discomfort	#7: State the Obvious	#14: Take Contrary Action
Disjointedness	#13: Ground	#7: State the Obvious
Extreme reactivity	#1: Breathe & Center	#12: Contain
Flakiness	#13: Ground	#14: Take Contrary Action
Flightiness	#13: Ground	#15: Get into Action
Forgetfulness	#13: Ground	#14: Take Contrary Action
Hesitation	#7: State the Obvious	#8: Confront
Hyperactivity	#1: Breathe & Center	#9: Disengage
Impulsivity	#12: Contain	#14: Take Contrary Action
Intrusion	#12: Contain	#9: Disengage
Irritability	#6: Direct Statements	#12: Contain
Isolating	#5: Tell the Truth	#10: Show Up
Lateness	#6: Direct Statements	#14: Take Contrary Action

Lethargy	#15: Get into Action	#6: Direct Statements
Lying	#5: Tell the Truth	#10: Show Up
Nervousness	#1: Breathe & Center	#12: Contain
Over-analyzing	#11: Thought Stop	#10: Show Up
Panic	#1: Breathe & Center	#11: Thought Stop
People-pleasing	#5: Tell the Truth	#9: Disengage
Reluctance	#8: Confront	#10: Show Up
Sabotage	#15: Get into Action	#10: Show Up
Shyness	#7: State the Obvious	#8: Confront
Silence	#6: Direct Statements	#8: Confront
Snide remarks	#6: Direct Statements	#12: Contain
Talkativeness	#1: Breathe & Center	#12: Contain
Tantrums	#6: Direct Statements	#12: Contain
Vigilance	#11: Thought Stop	#14: Take Contrary Action
Whining	#6: Direct Statements	#15: Get into action

APPENDIX D
HEALING PATHWAYS

Gain freedom from crippling defenses by walking the pathway laid out in this workbook and in <u>Stuck in the Story No More</u> *(the foundational book on which this workbook is based). First use the Defense Profiles in* <u>Stuck in the Story No More</u> *to identify your defensive patterns. Then apply the Defense Detectors, Defense Alternatives, and Defense Resources in this workbook. Page numbers for the Defense Profiles show below refer to* <u>Stuck in the Story No More</u>. *Other numbers refer to pages in this workbook.*

Healing Pathway for:	Defense Profile	Defense Detectors	Defense Alternatives	Defense Resources
Analyzing as a defense	p. 129	p. 21	p. 101	p. 151
Anger as a defense	p. 65	p. 7	p. 81	p. 144
Blame as a defense	p. 75	p. 9	p. 84	p. 145
Chaos as a defense	p. 180	p. 31	p. 116	p. 156
Codependence as a defense	p. 96	p. 14	p. 91	p. 147
Comparing as a defense	p. 125	p. 20	p. 100	p. 150
Compulsivity as a defense	p. 183	p. 32	p. 118	p. 156
Confusion as a defense	p. 216	p. 40	p. 129	p. 160
Contempt for Others as a defense	p. 72	p. 8	p. 83	p. 144
Control as a defense	p. 105	p. 16	p. 94	p. 148
Counter-Dependence as a defense	p. 187	p. 33	p. 119	p. 157
Criticism as a defense	p. 109	p. 17	p. 96	p. 149
Denial as a defense	p. 222	p. 42	p. 132	p. 161
Dependence as a defense	p. 90	p. 13	p. 90	p. 147
Depression as a defense	p. 165	p. 28	p. 112	p. 154
Dissociation as a defense	p. 202	p. 37	p. 125	p. 159
Fantasy as a defense	p. 237	p. 46	p. 137	p. 163

Healing Pathway for:	Defense Profile	Defense Detectors	Defense Alternatives	Defense Resources
Fear as a defense	p. 149	p. 25	p. 107	p. 153
Gossip as a defense	p. 82	p. 11	p. 87	p. 146
Guilt as a defense	p. 212	p. 39	p. 128	p. 160
Humor as a defense	p. 85	p. 12	p. 88	p. 146
Intellectualization as a defense	p. 219	p. 41	p. 130	p. 161
Judgment as a defense	p. 122	p. 19	p. 99	p. 150
Masking as a defense	p. 133	p. 22	p. 103	p. 151
Obsession as a defense	p. 228	p. 44	p. 134	p. 162
Paranoia as a defense	p. 208	p. 38	p. 126	p. 159
Perfectionism as a defense	p. 241	p. 47	p. 139	p. 164
Physical Illness as a defense	p. 197	p. 36	p. 123	p. 158
Procrastination as a defense	p. 190	p. 34	p. 121	p. 157
Projection as a defense	p. 115	p. 18	p. 97	p. 149
Self-Absorption as a defense	p. 232	p. 45	p. 136	p. 163
Self-Contempt as a defense	p. 145	p. 24	p. 106	p. 152
Shame as a defense	p. 139	p. 23	p. 104	p. 152
Skepticism as a defense	p. 225	p. 43	p. 133	p. 162
Spilling as a defense	p. 79	p. 10	p. 86	p. 145
Spirituality as a defense	p. 174	p. 30	p. 115	p. 155
Terminal Uniqueness as a defense	p. 170	p. 29	p. 113	p. 155
Therapizing as a defense	p. 101	p. 15	p. 93	p. 148
Victim as a defense	p. 156	p. 26	p. 109	p. 153
Withdrawal as a defense	p. 161	p. 27	p. 110	p. 154
Withholding as a defense	p. 194	p. 35	p. 122	p. 158

MY PERSONAL NOTES & OBSERVATIONS

MY PERSONAL NOTES & OBSERVATIONS

MY PERSONAL NOTES & OBSERVATIONS

MY PERSONAL NOTES & OBSERVATIONS

MY PERSONAL NOTES & OBSERVATIONS

MY PERSONAL NOTES & OBSERVATIONS